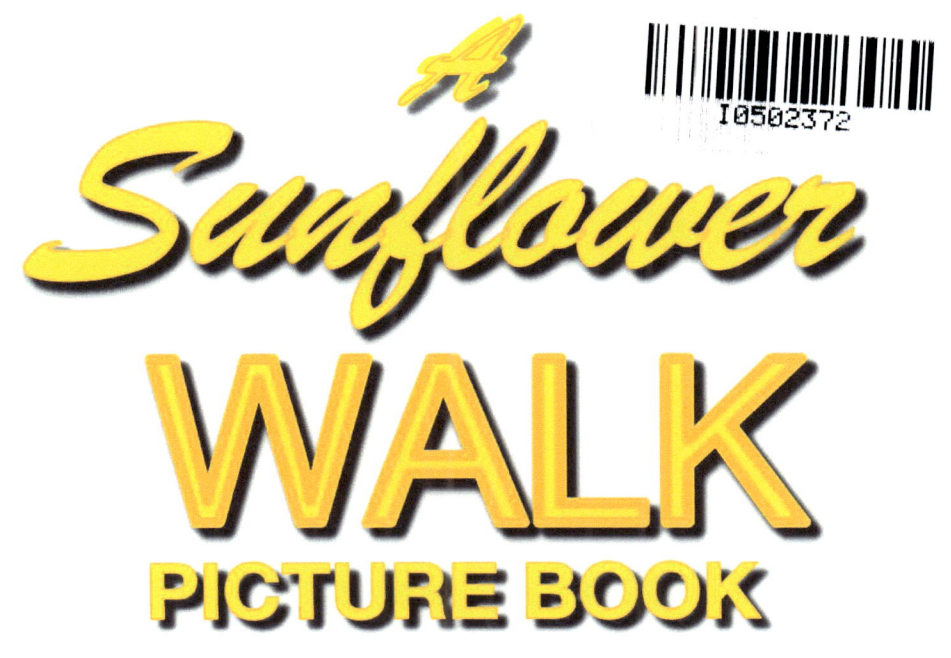

Mister E Press

Photos and text by Peter Evans.

NO A.I.

If you enjoyed reading this book, please consider adding a review to Amazon.

ISBN-13:9798343049190

No part of this publication, or the characters within it, may be reproduced or distributed in any form or by any means without prior written consent from the author except for the use of brief quotations in a book review. (misterepress@gmail.com)

Copyright © 2024 Mister E Press
All rights reserved.

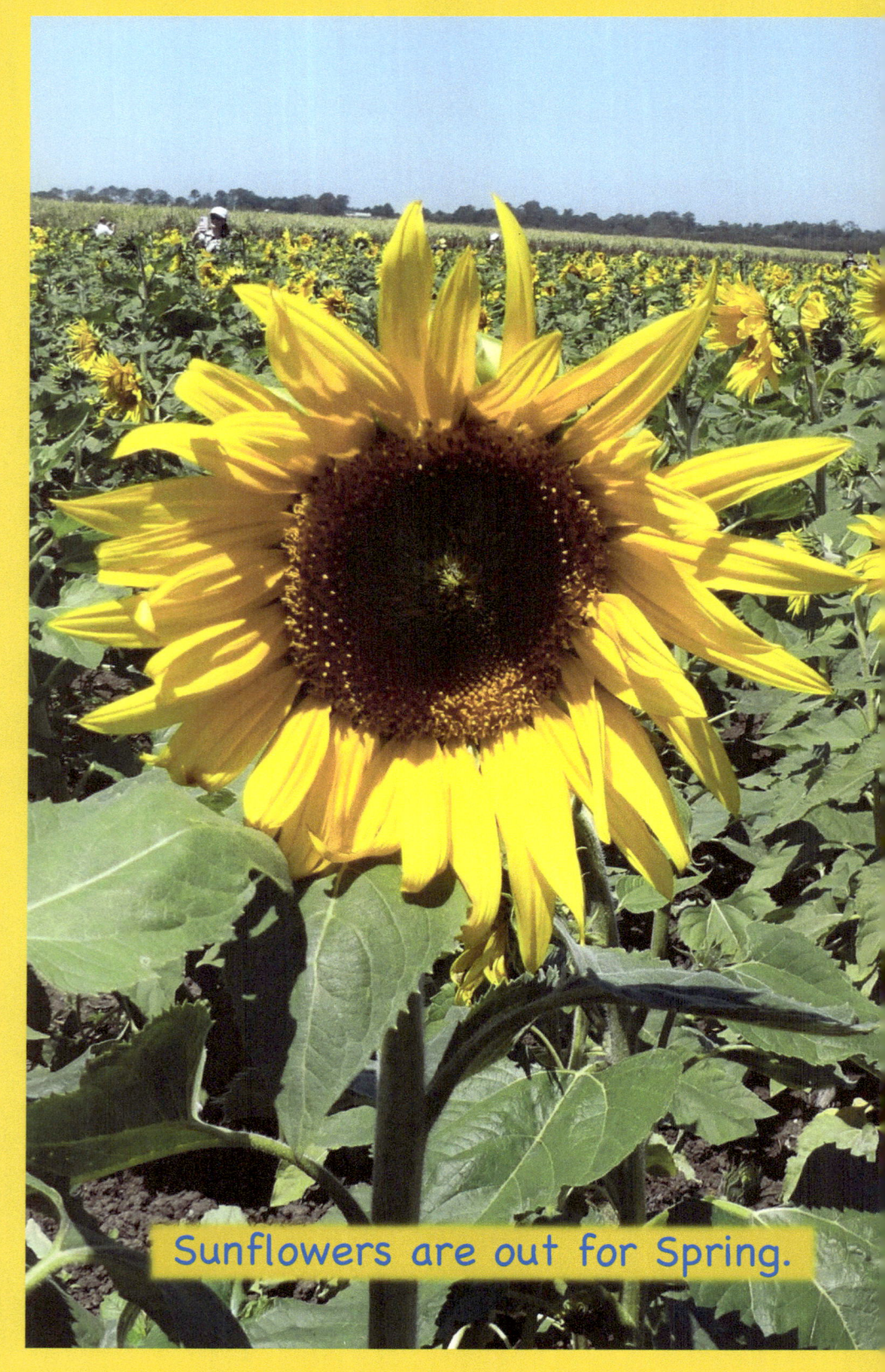
Sunflowers are out for Spring.

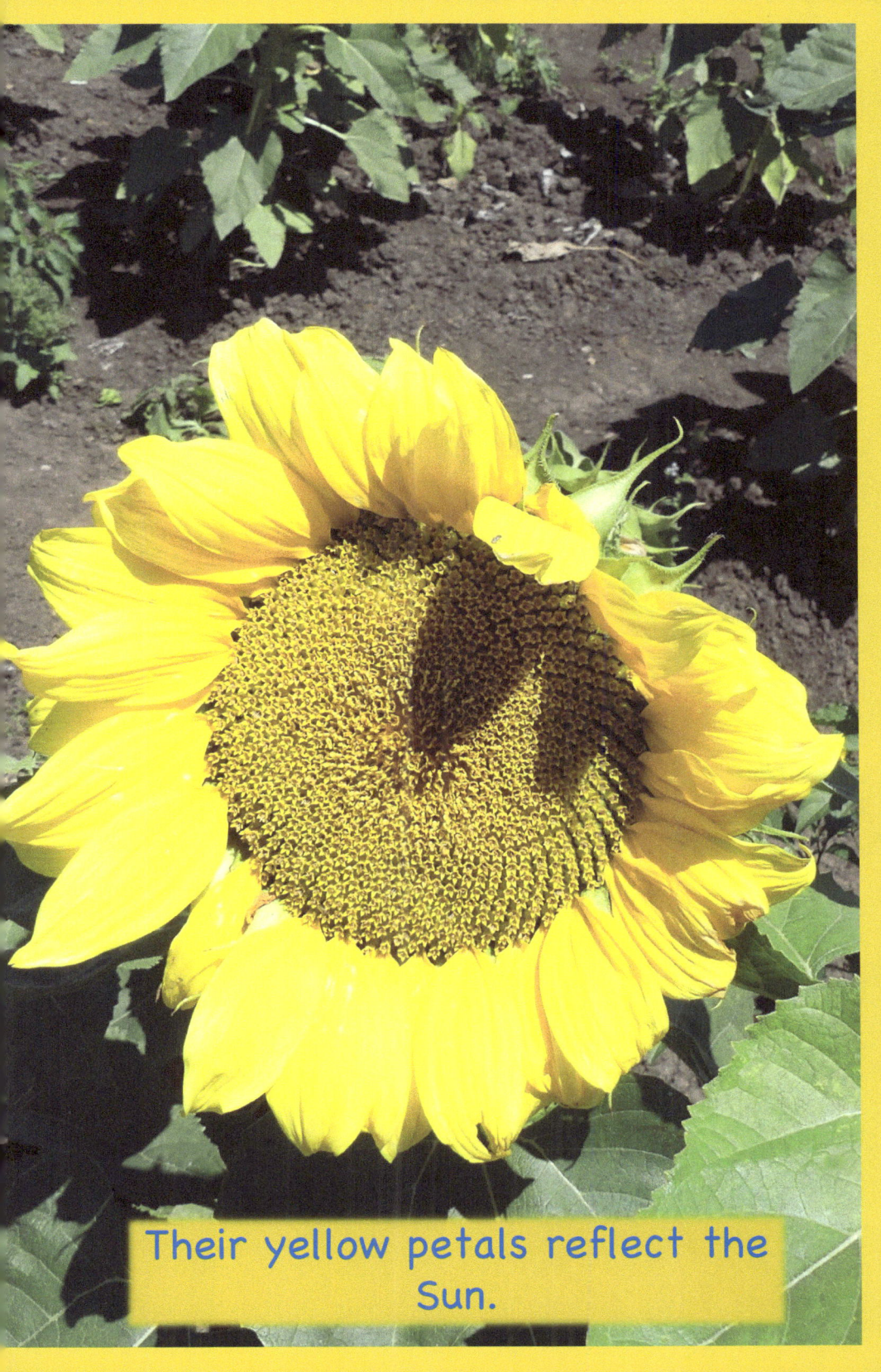

Their yellow petals reflect the Sun.

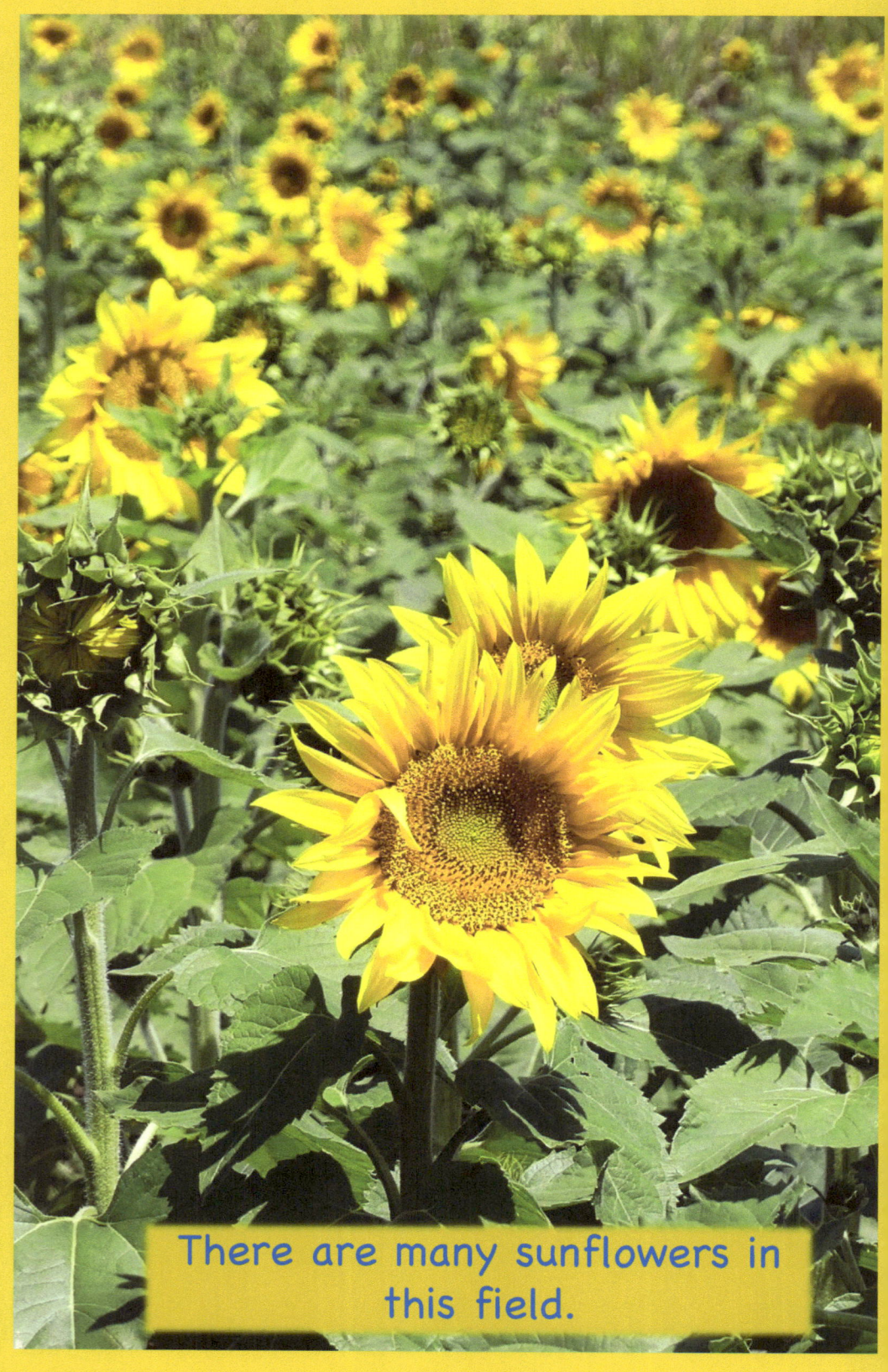
There are many sunflowers in this field.

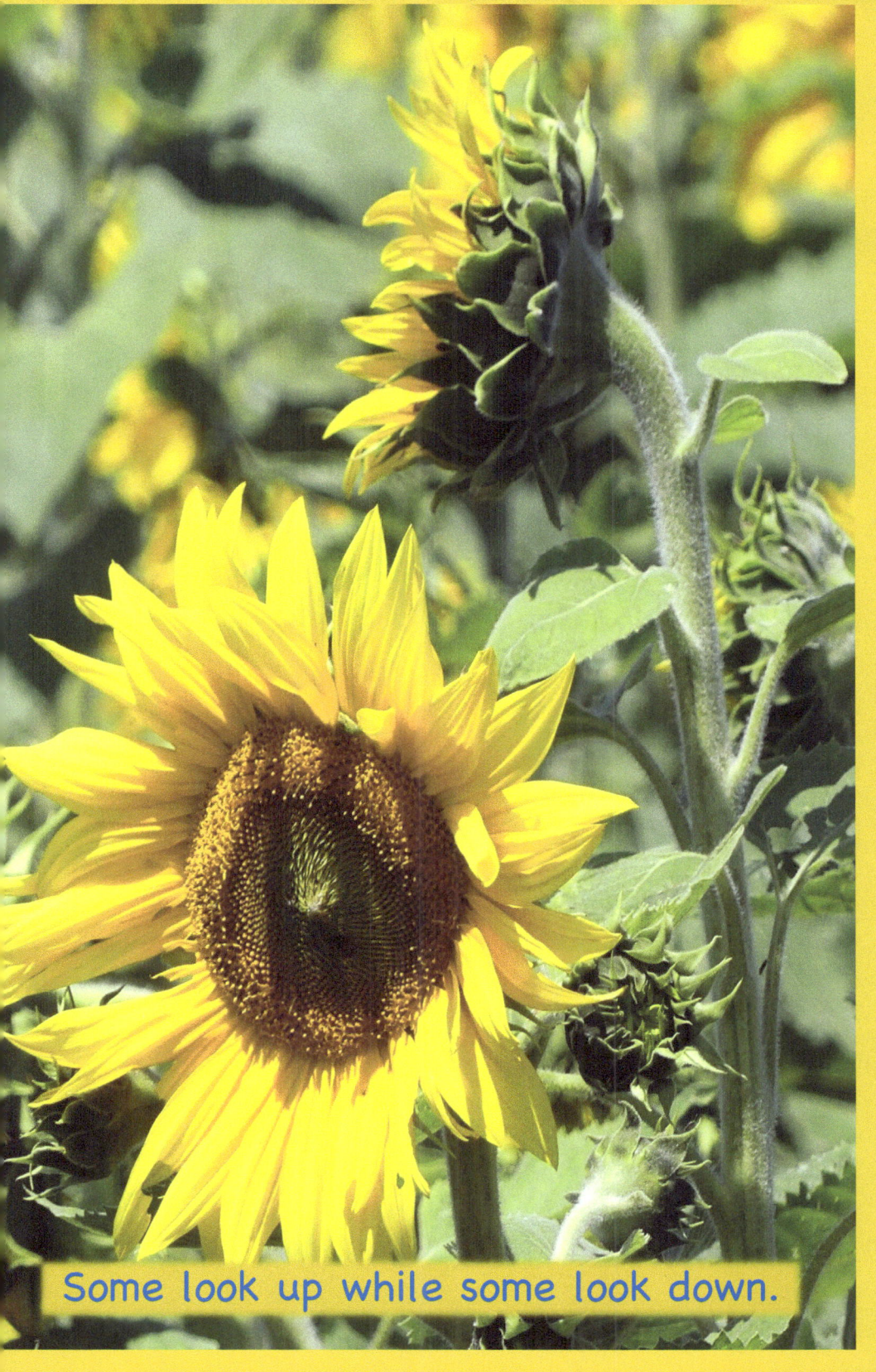
Some look up while some look down.

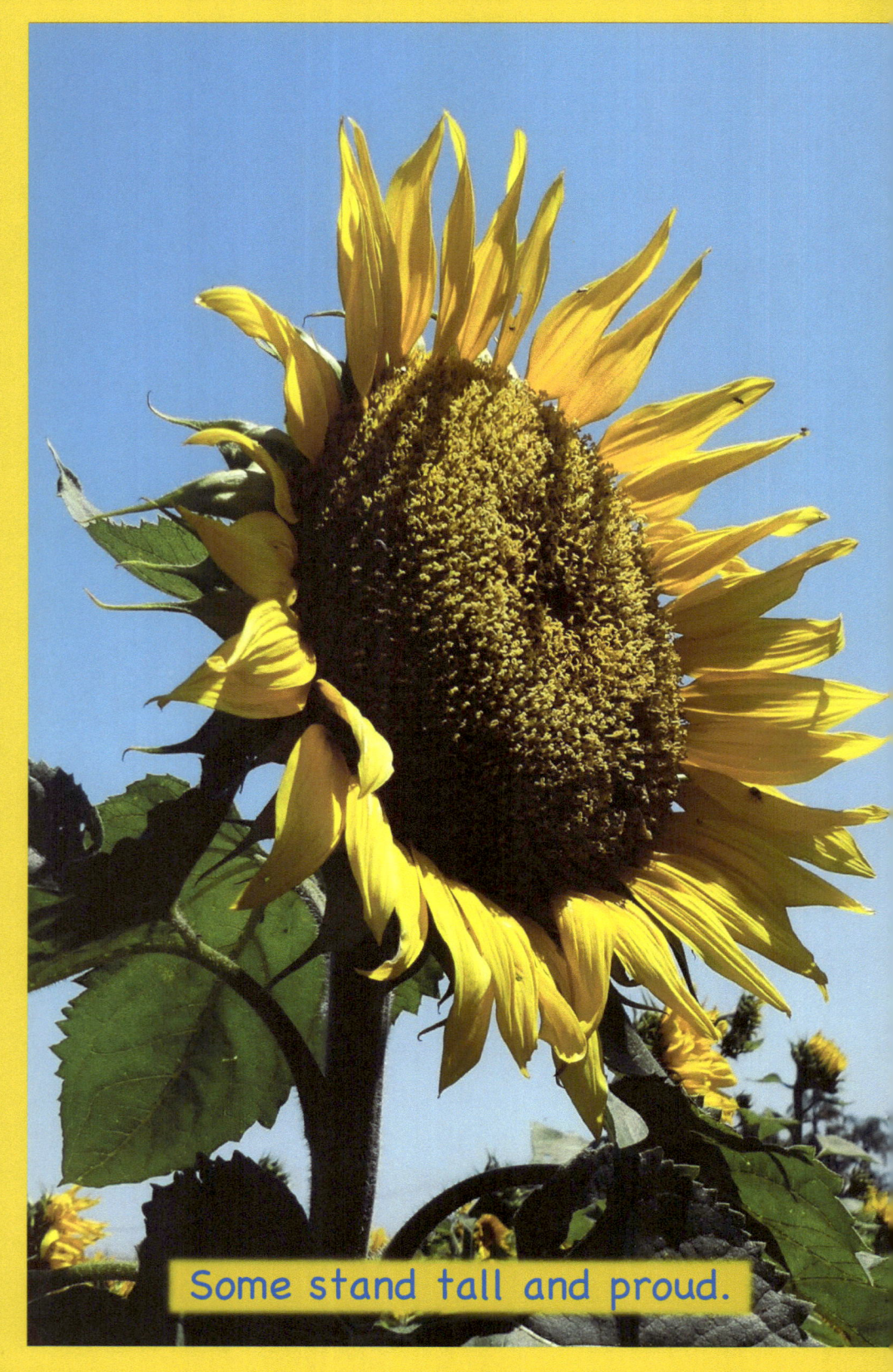
Some stand tall and proud.

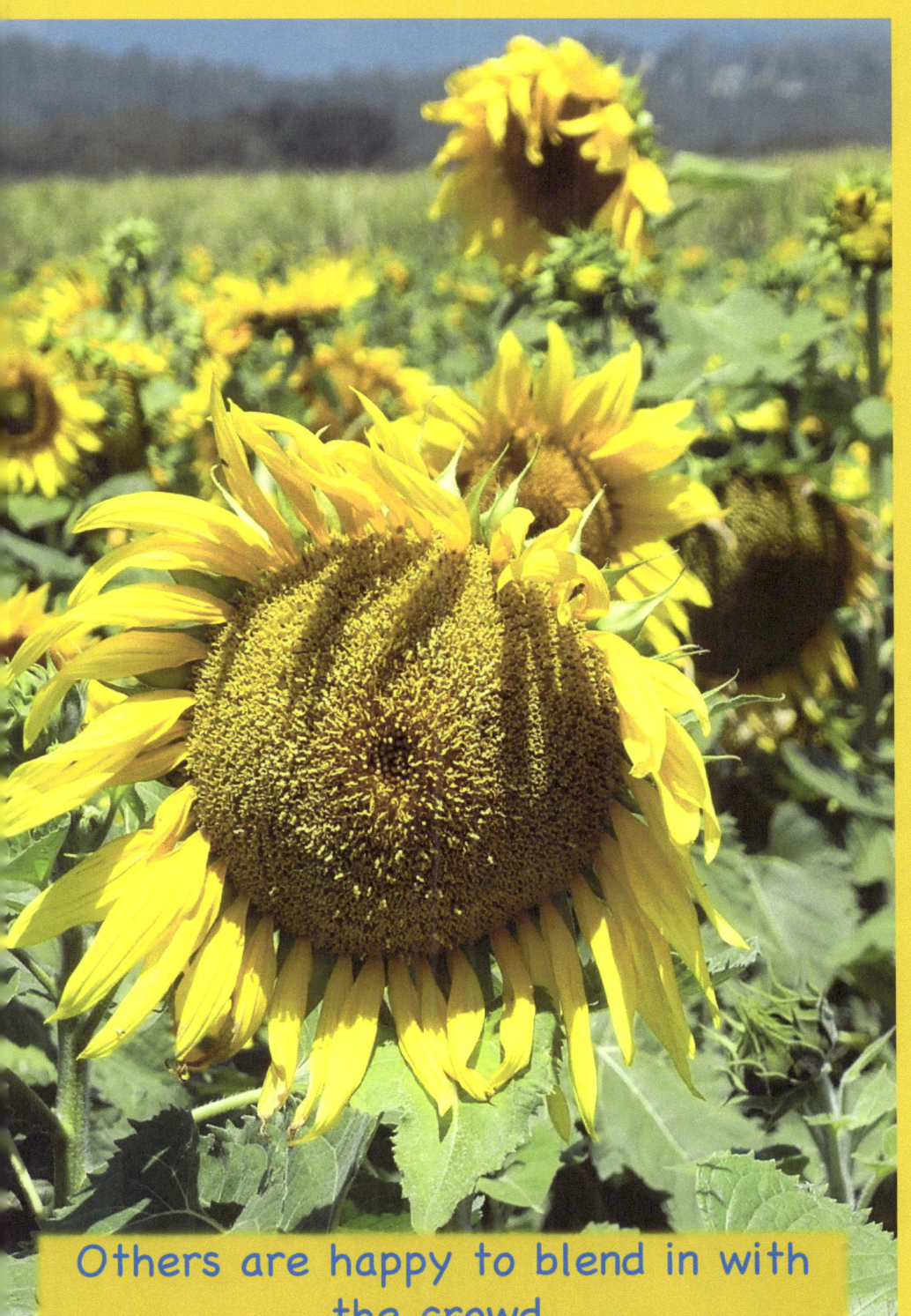

Others are happy to blend in with the crowd.

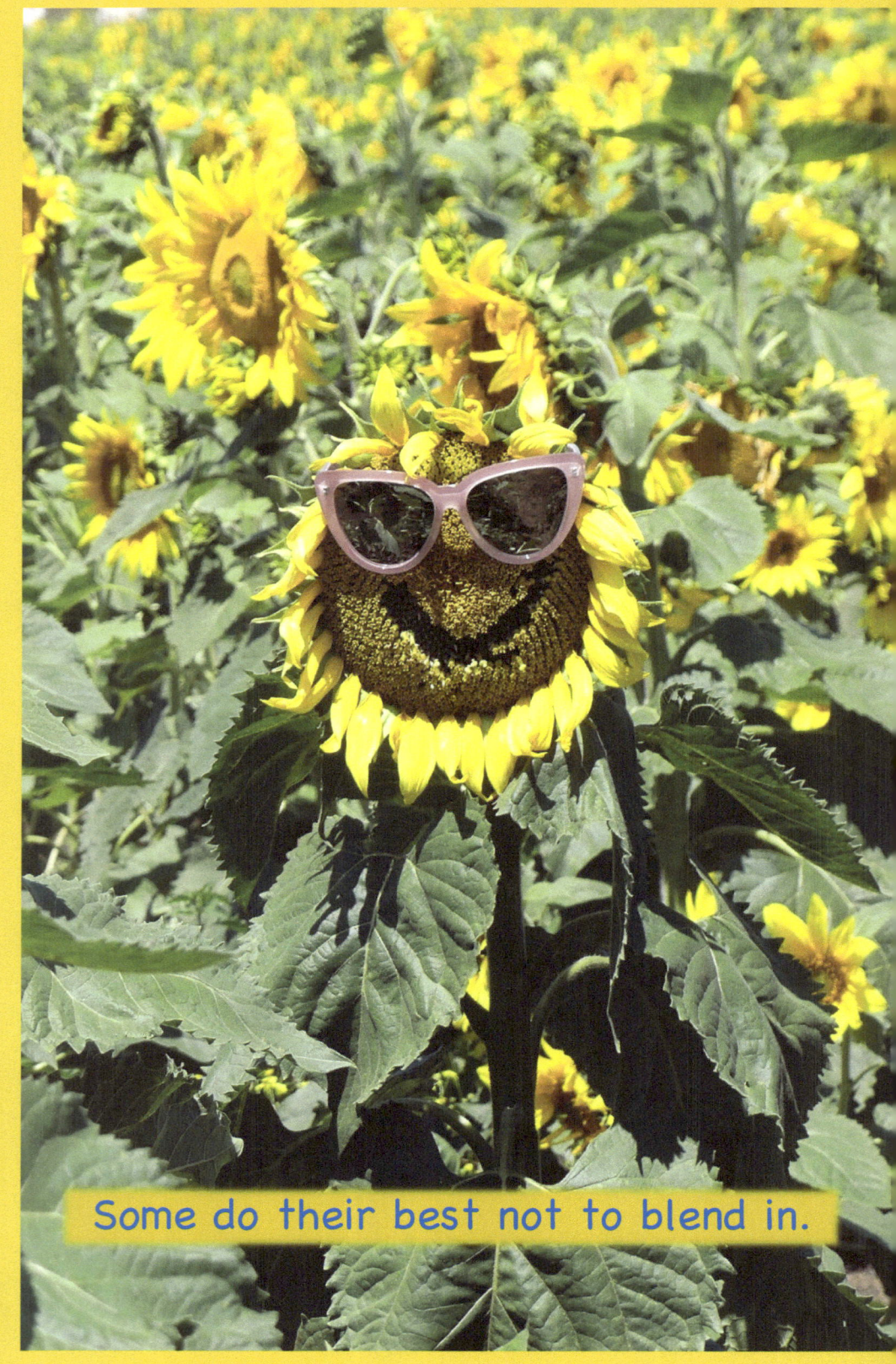
Some do their best not to blend in.

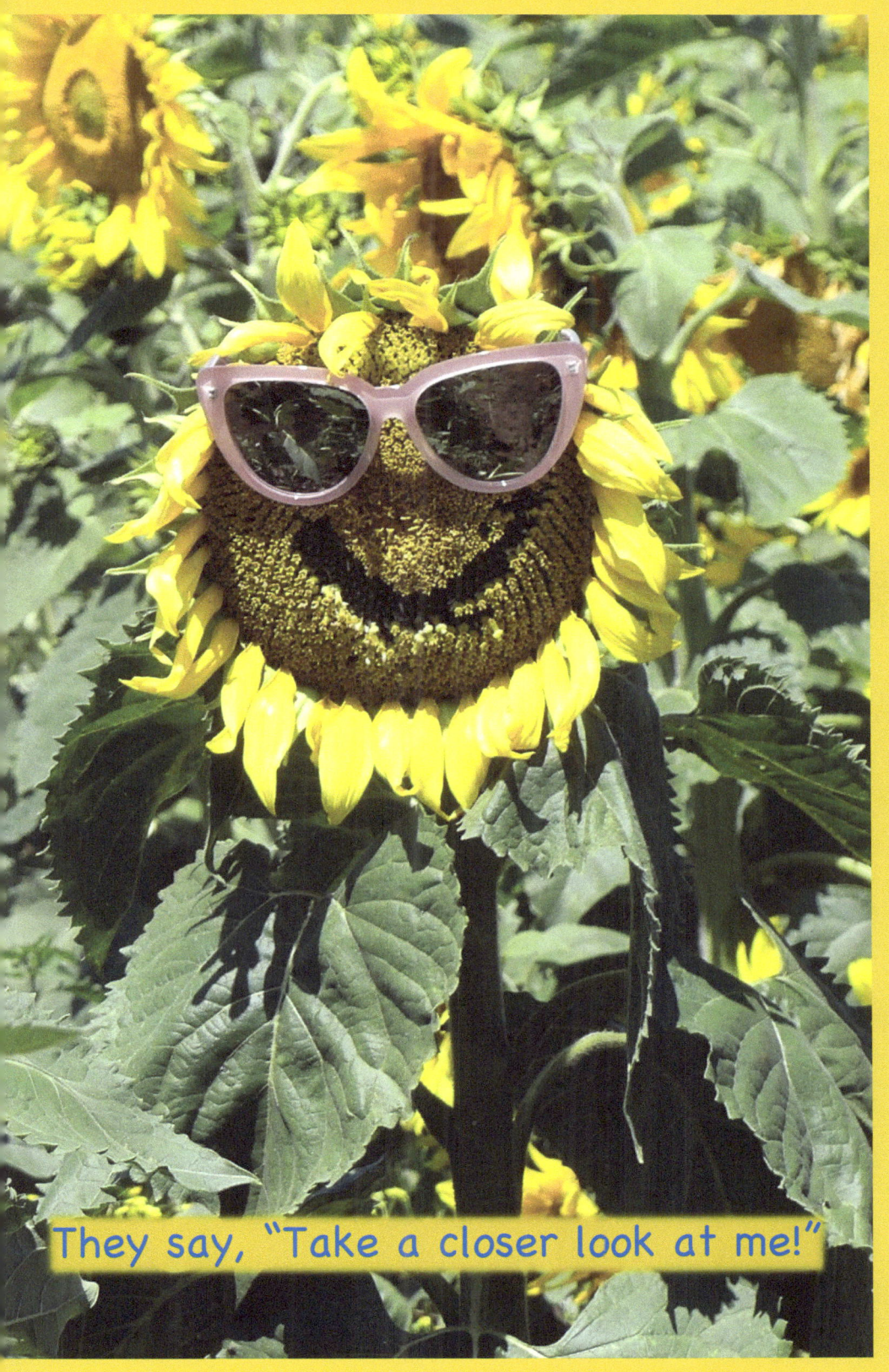
They say, "Take a closer look at me!"

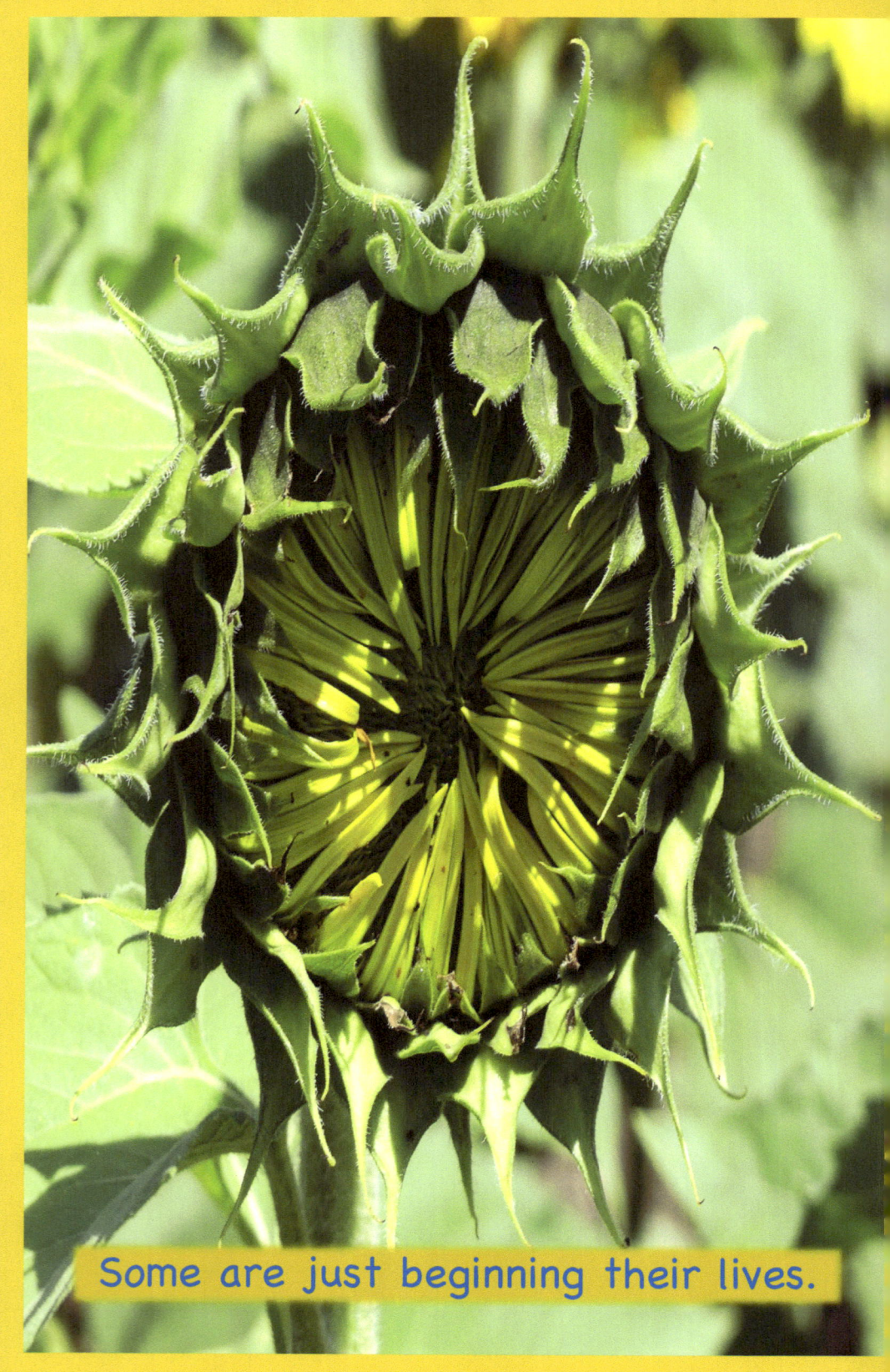

Some are just beginning their lives.

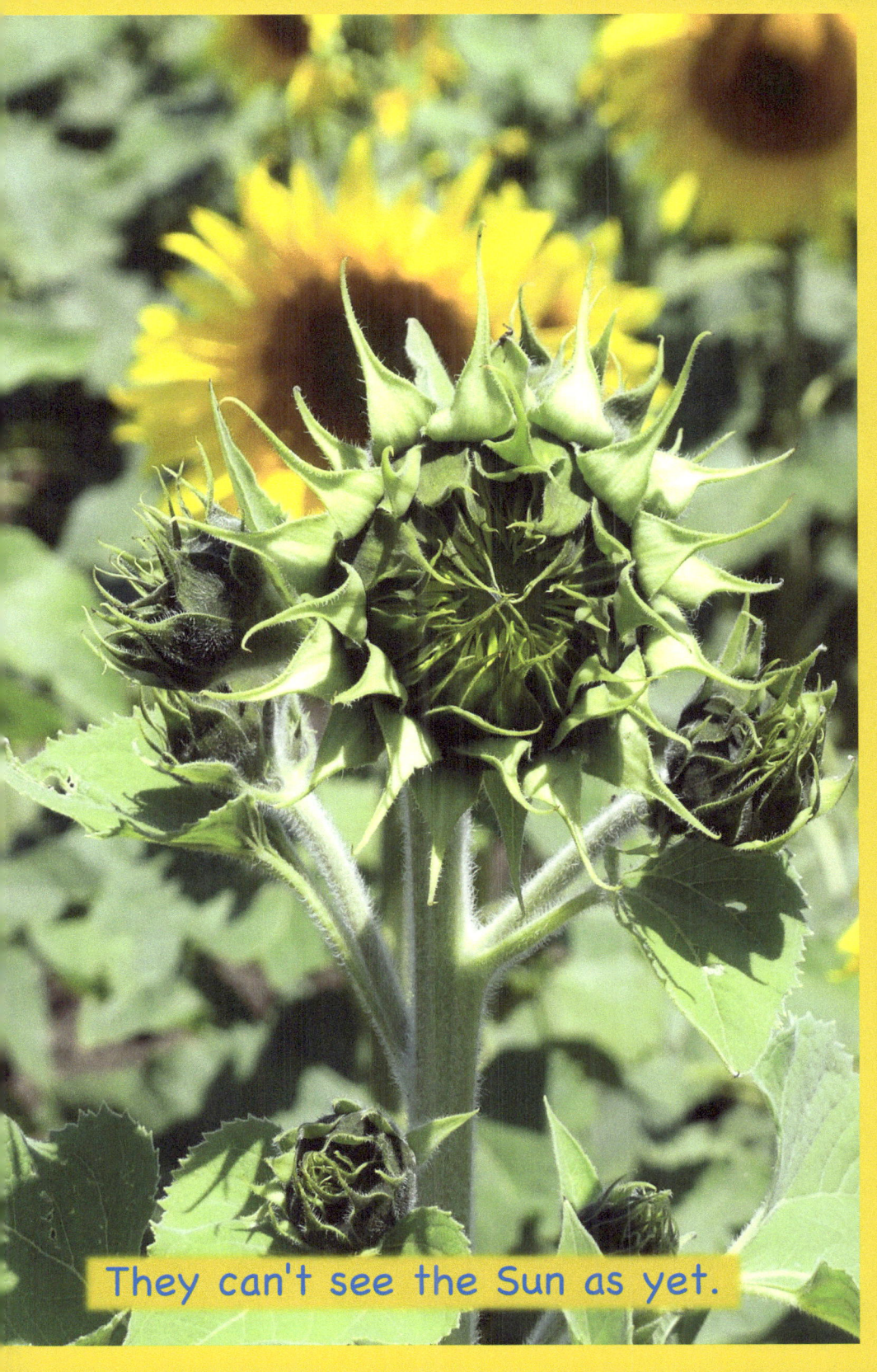
They can't see the Sun as yet.

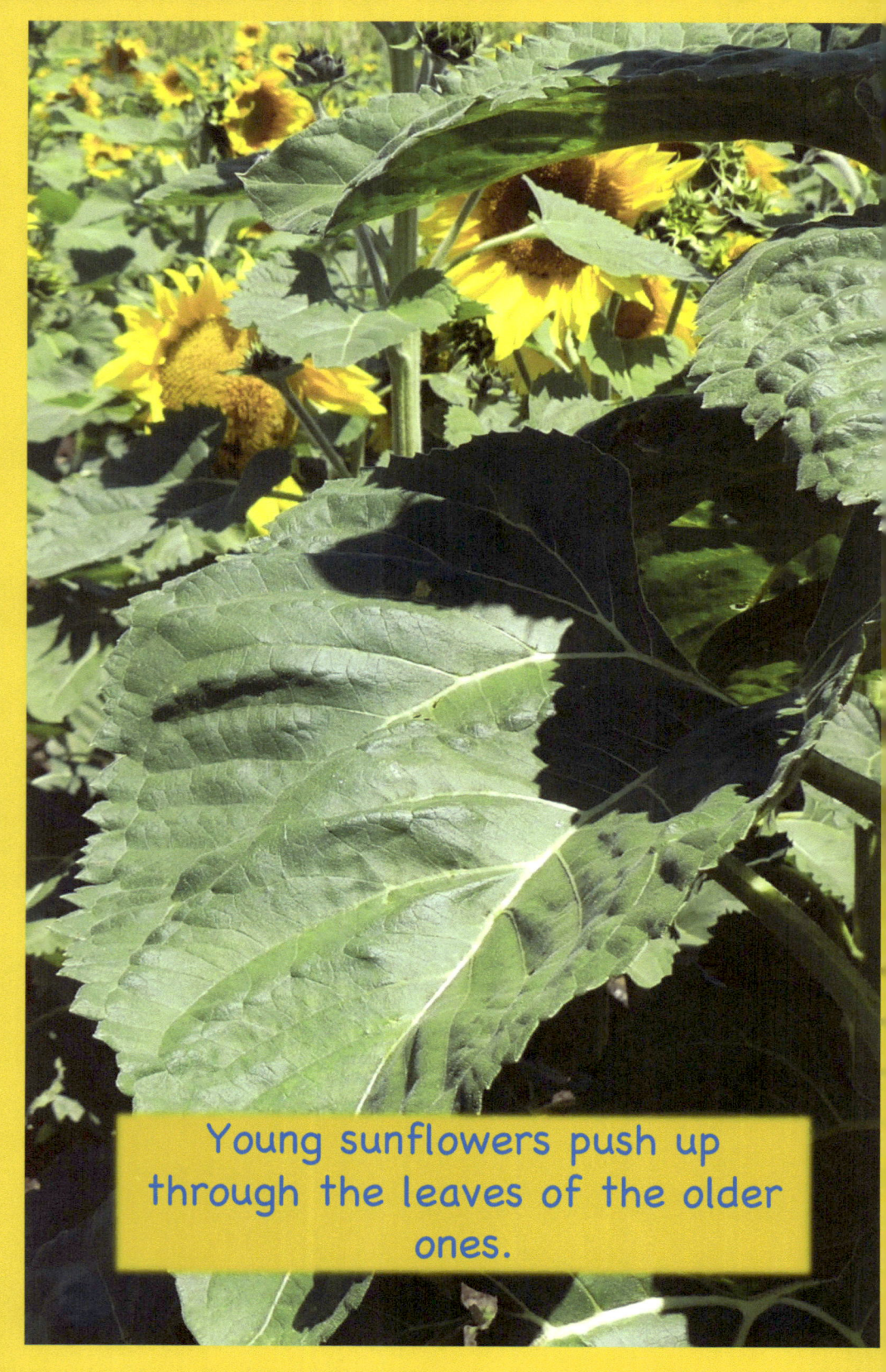
Young sunflowers push up through the leaves of the older ones.

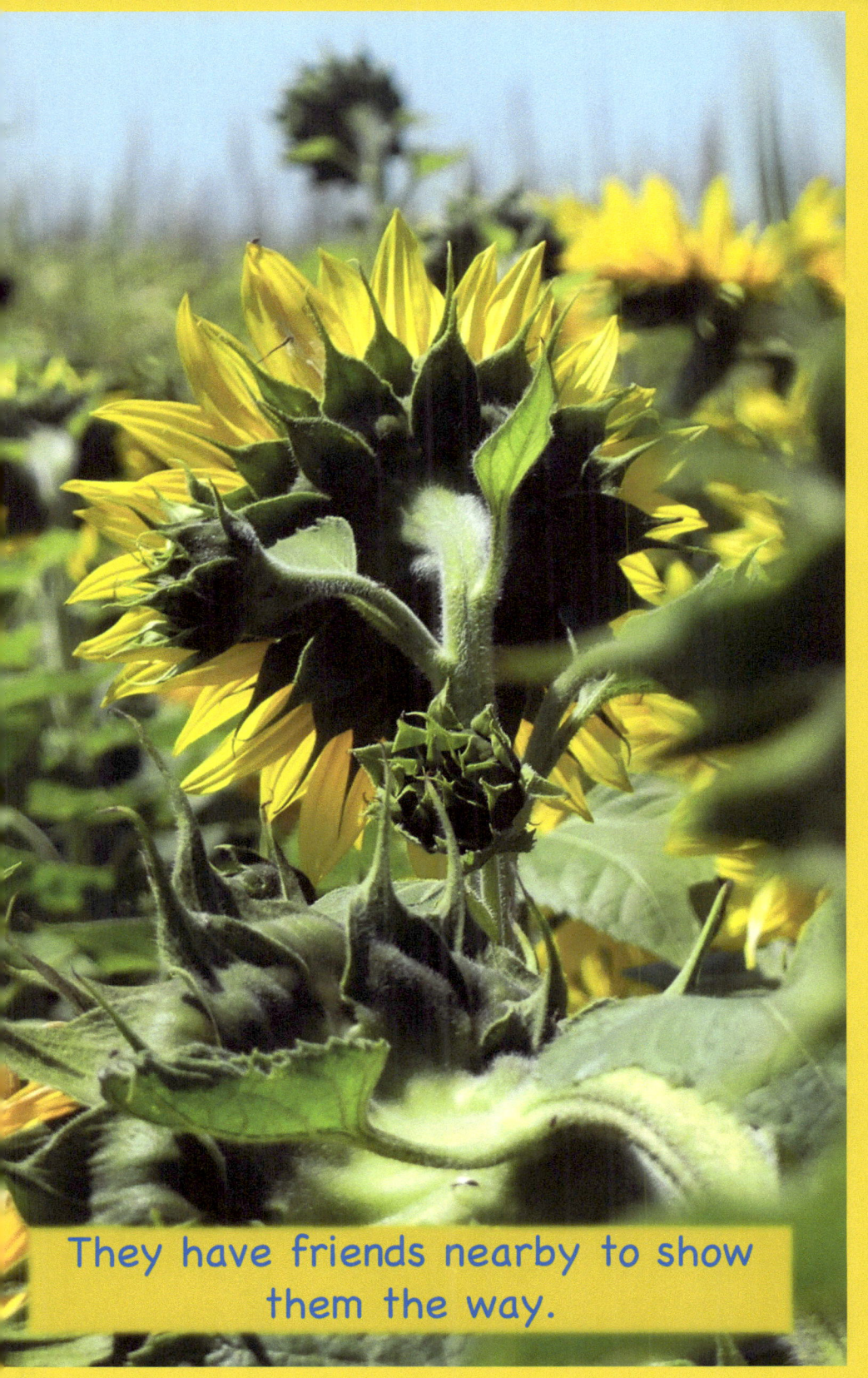

They have friends nearby to show them the way.

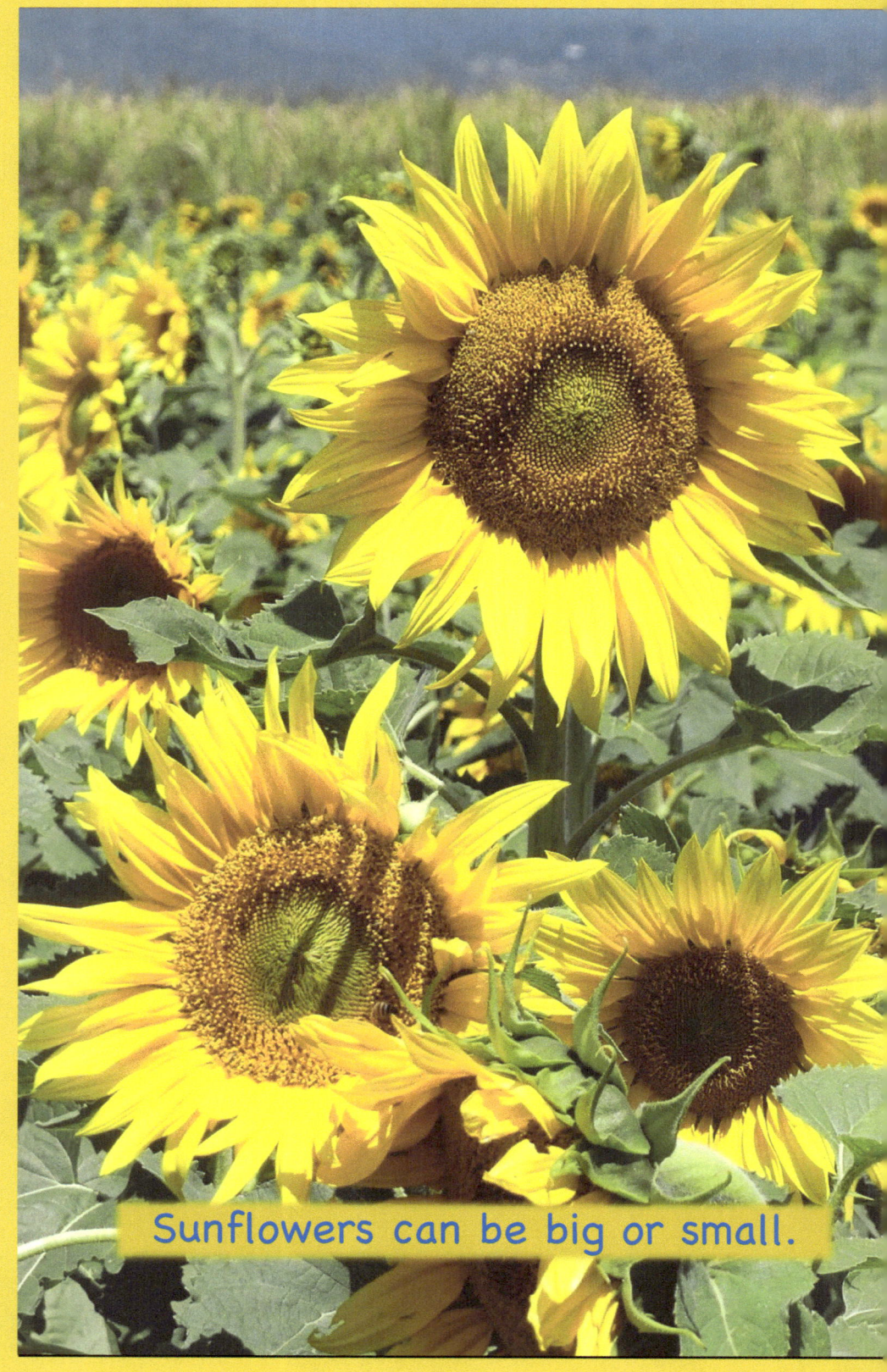

Sunflowers can be big or small.

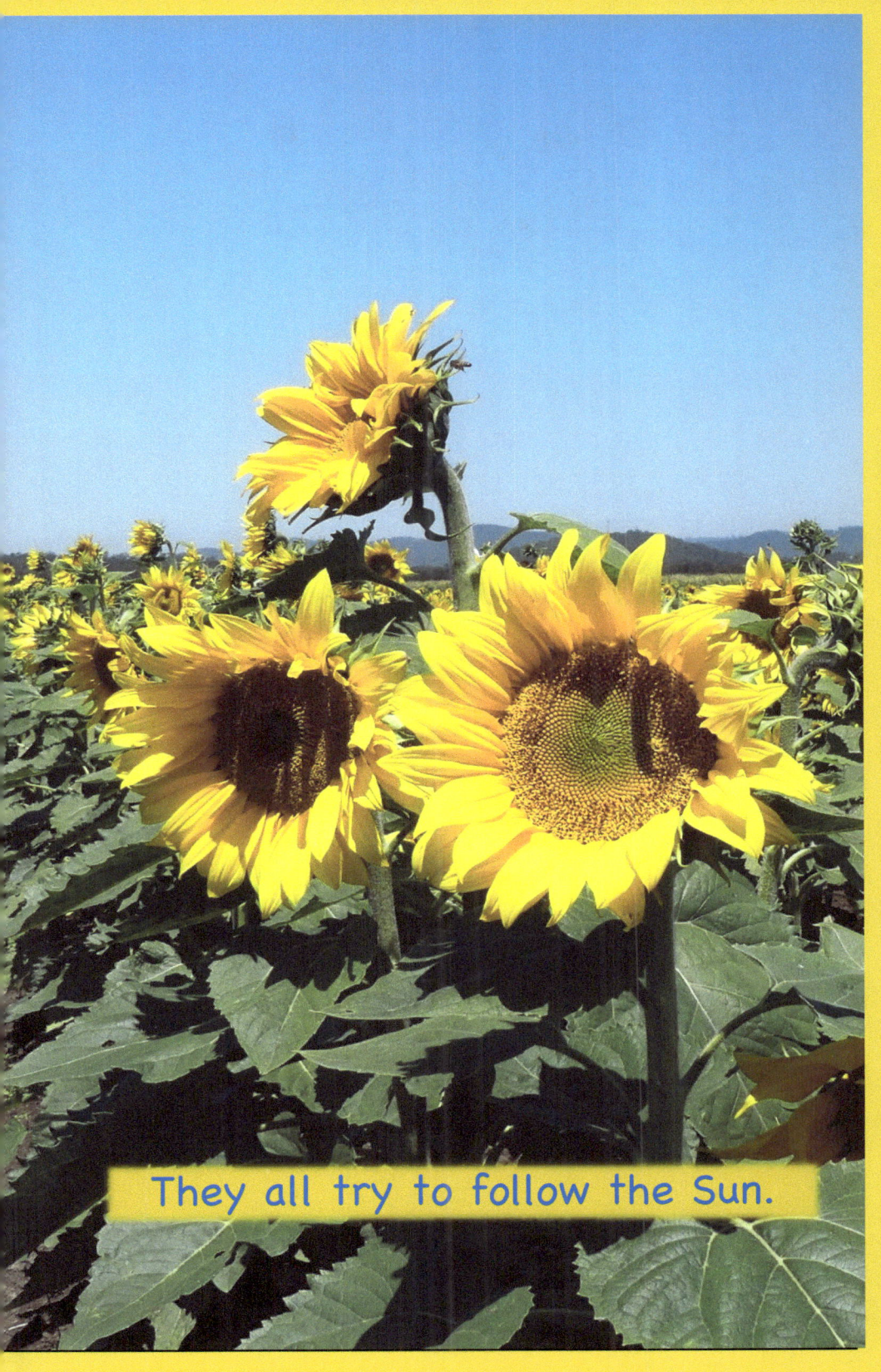
They all try to follow the Sun.

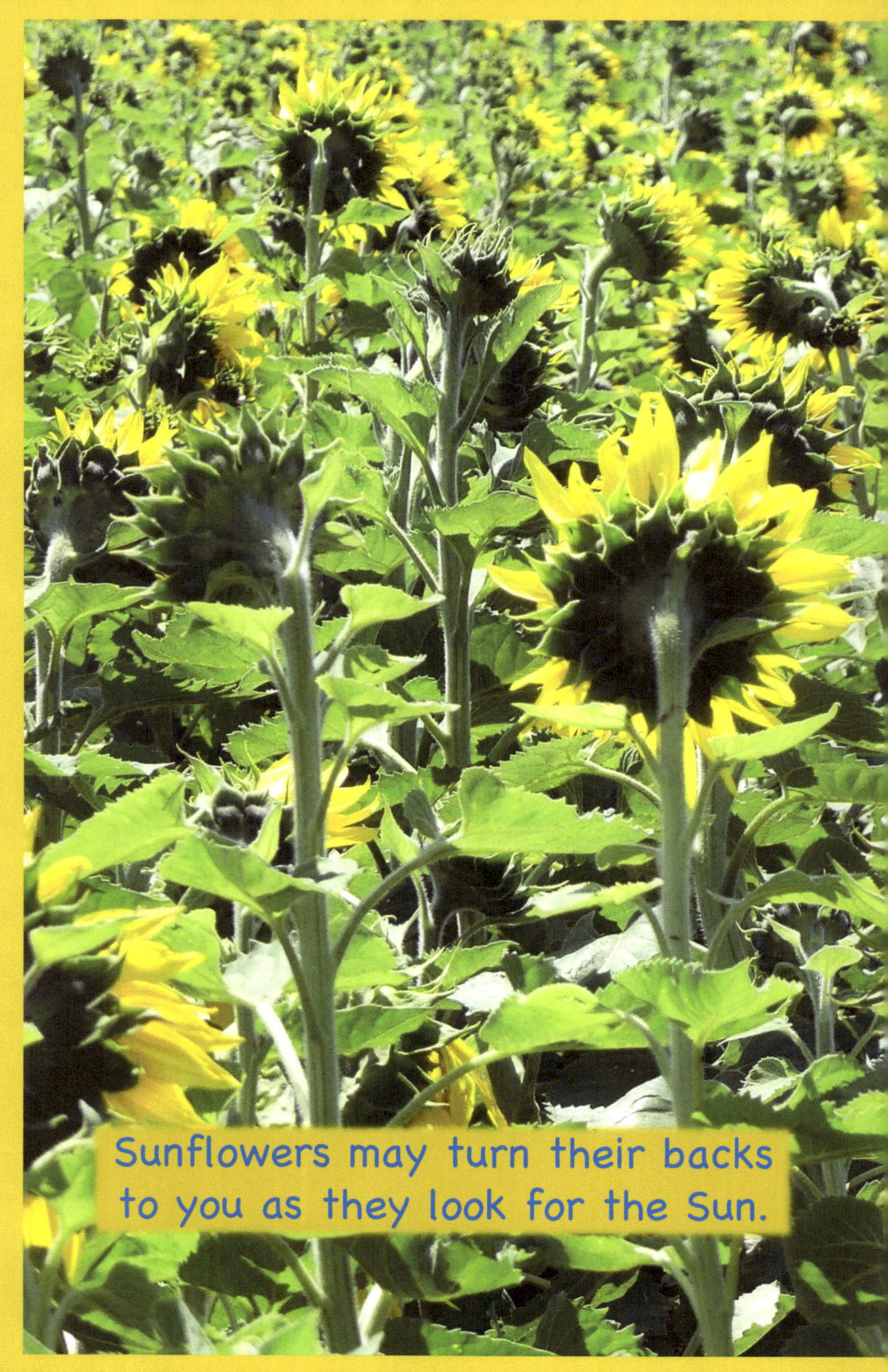
Sunflowers may turn their backs to you as they look for the Sun.

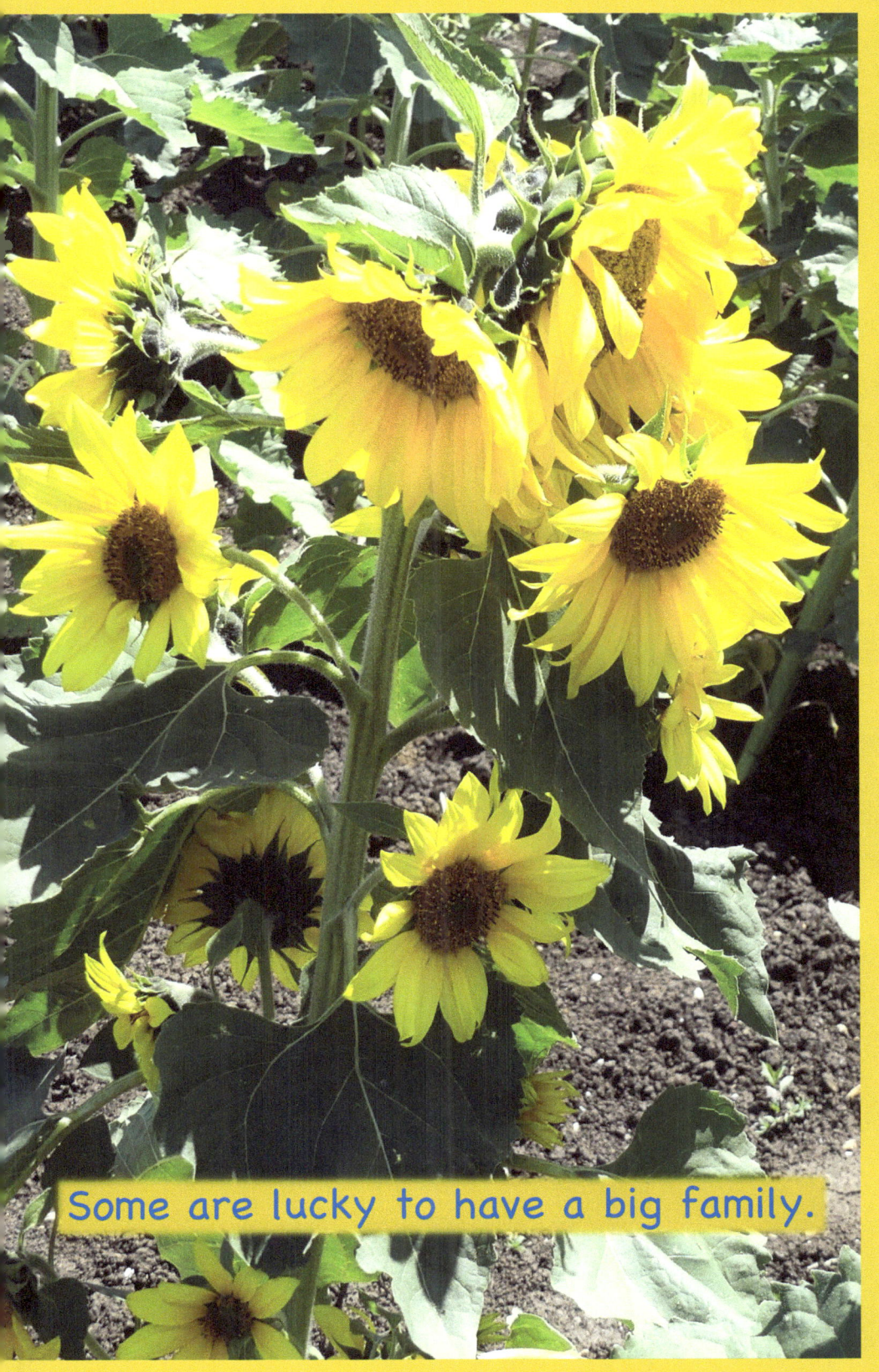

Some are lucky to have a big family.

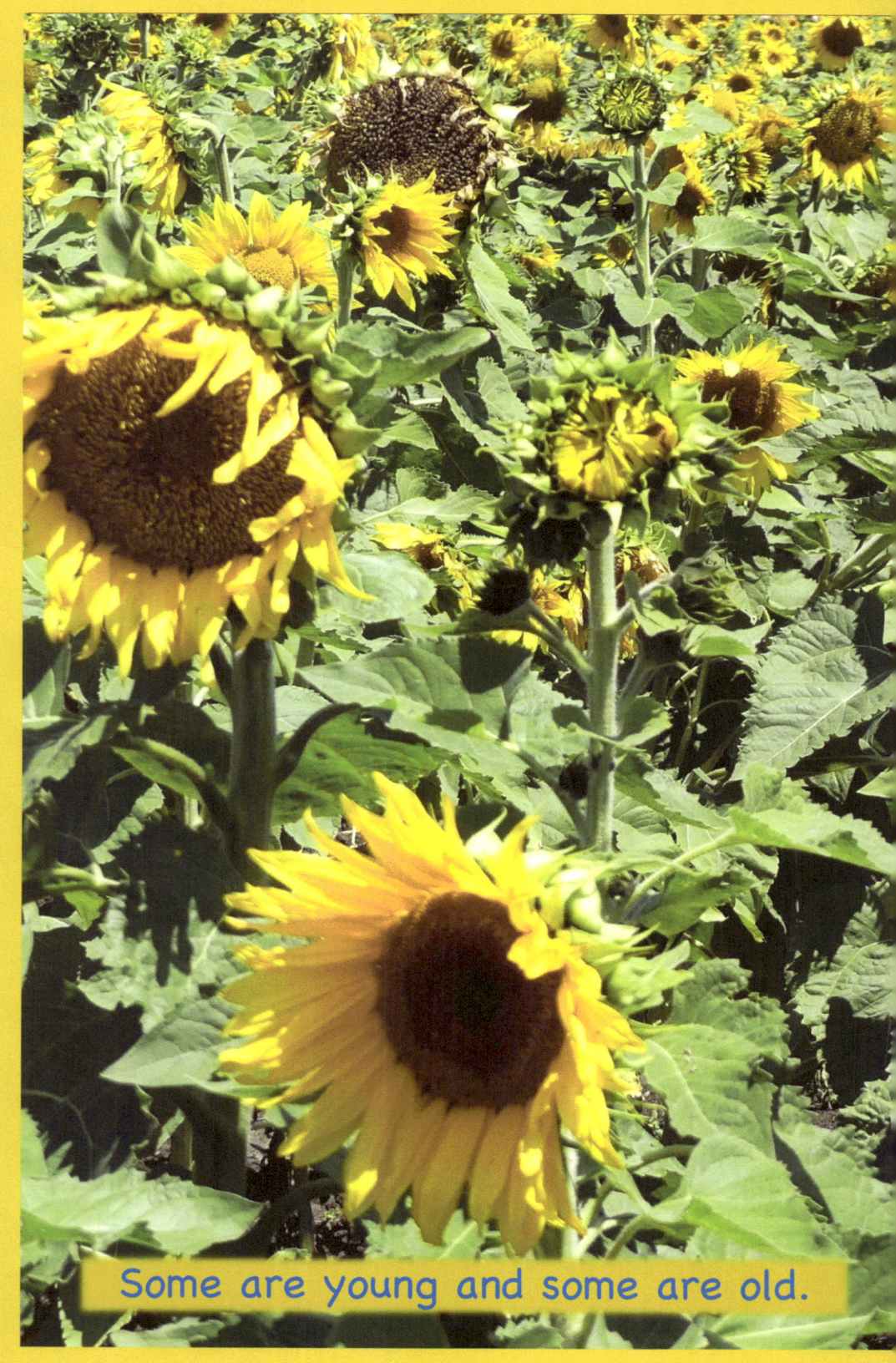

Some are young and some are old.

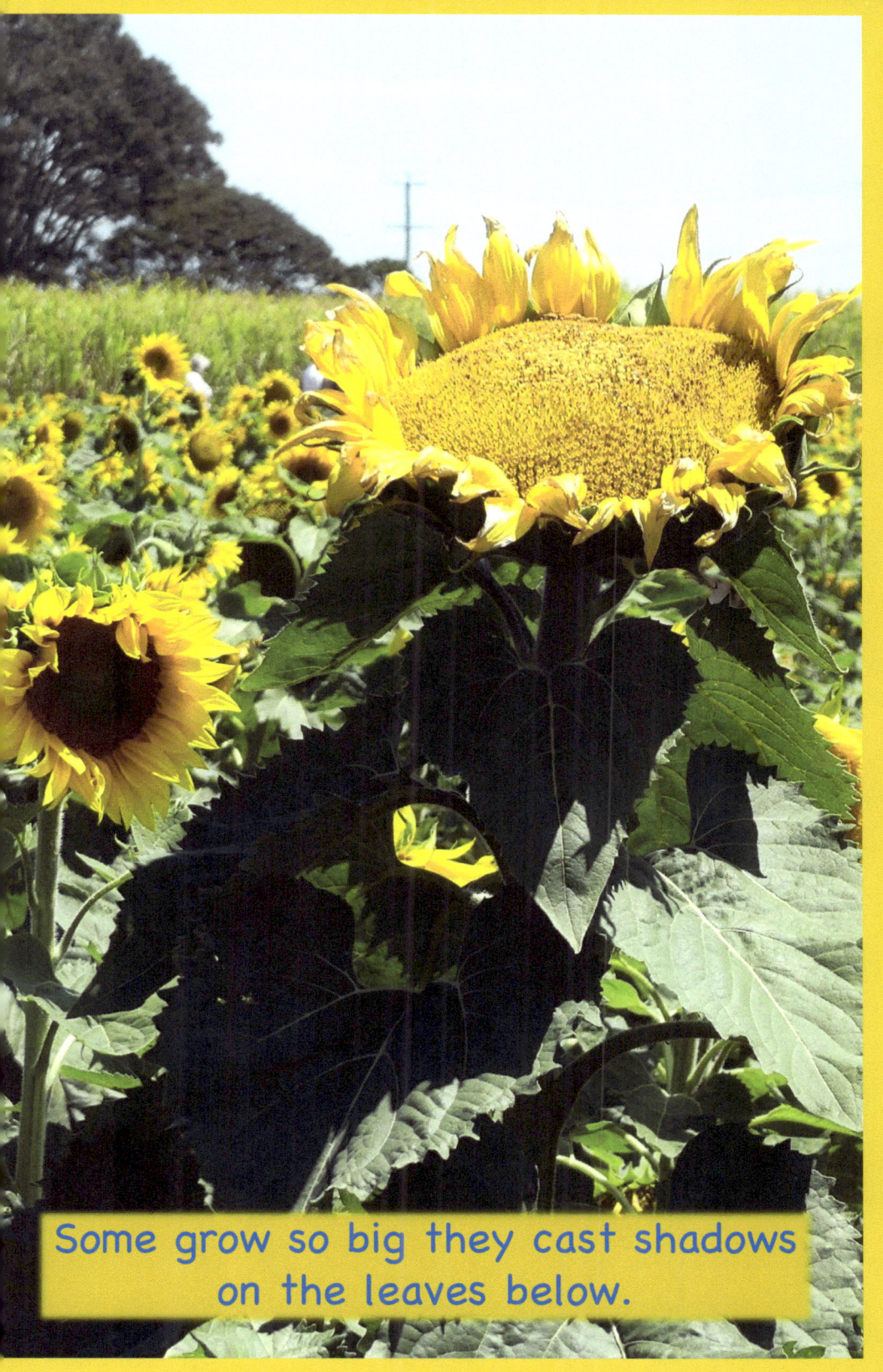
Some grow so big they cast shadows on the leaves below.

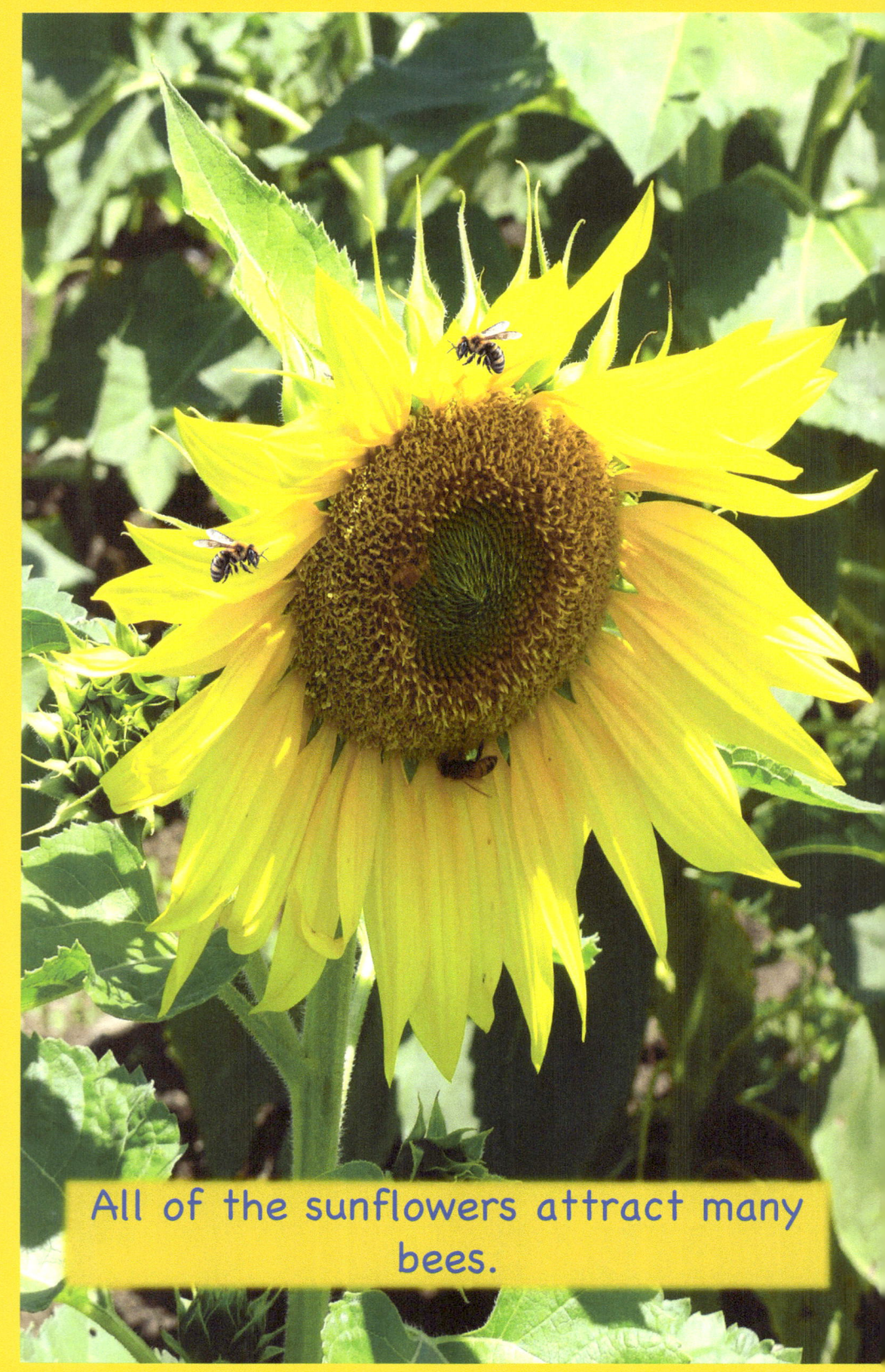

All of the sunflowers attract many bees.

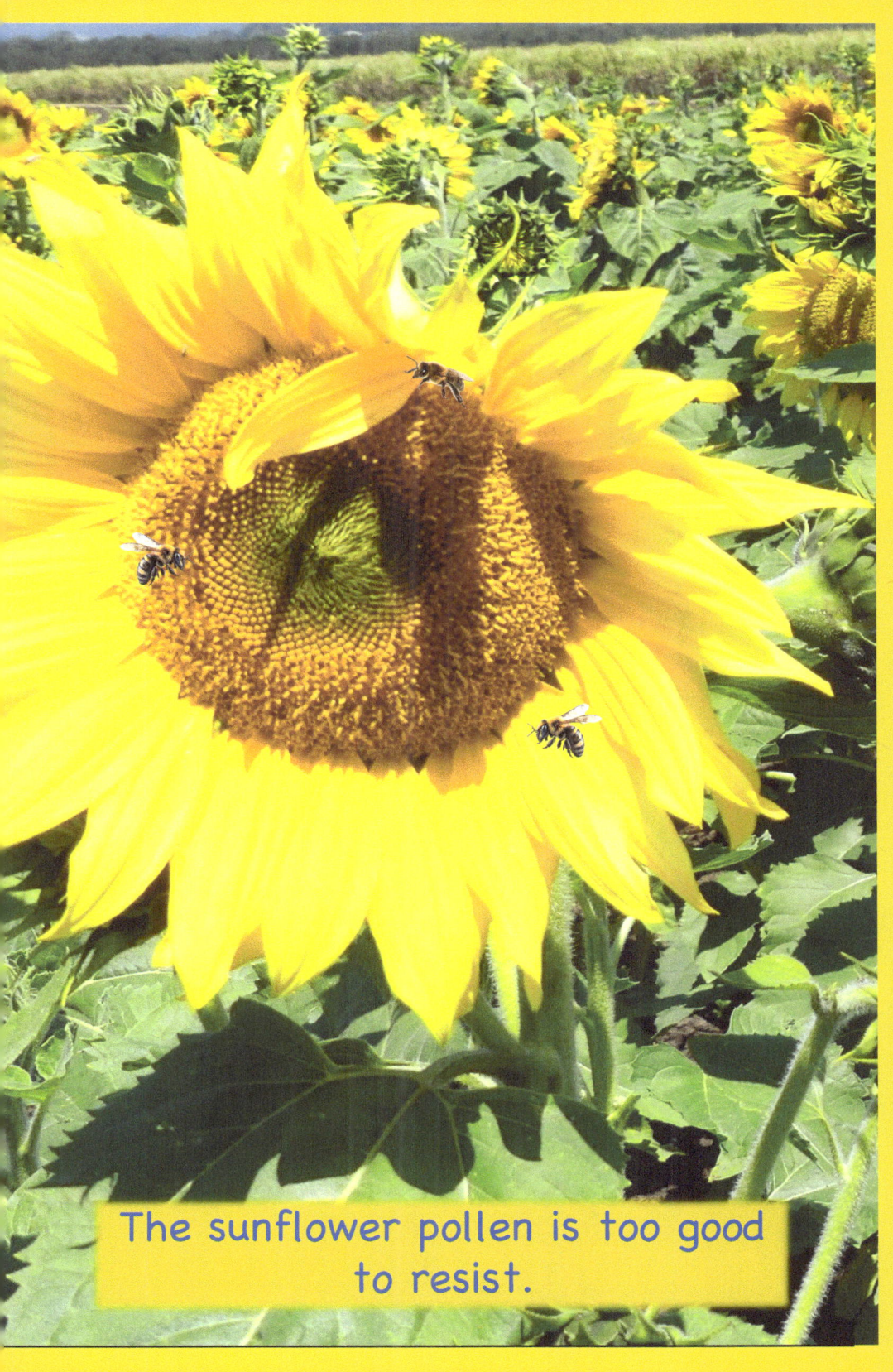

The sunflower pollen is too good to resist.

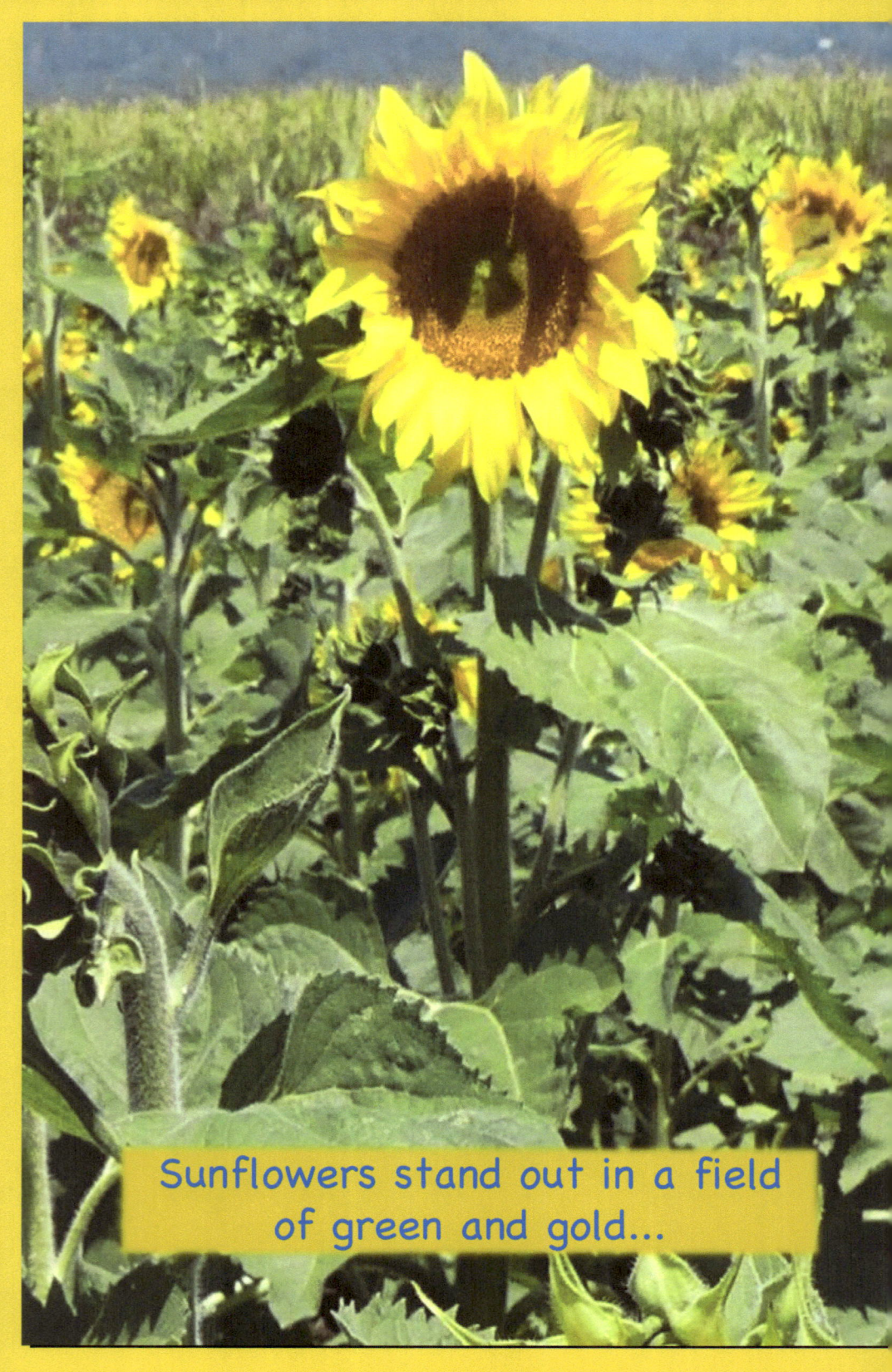
Sunflowers stand out in a field of green and gold...

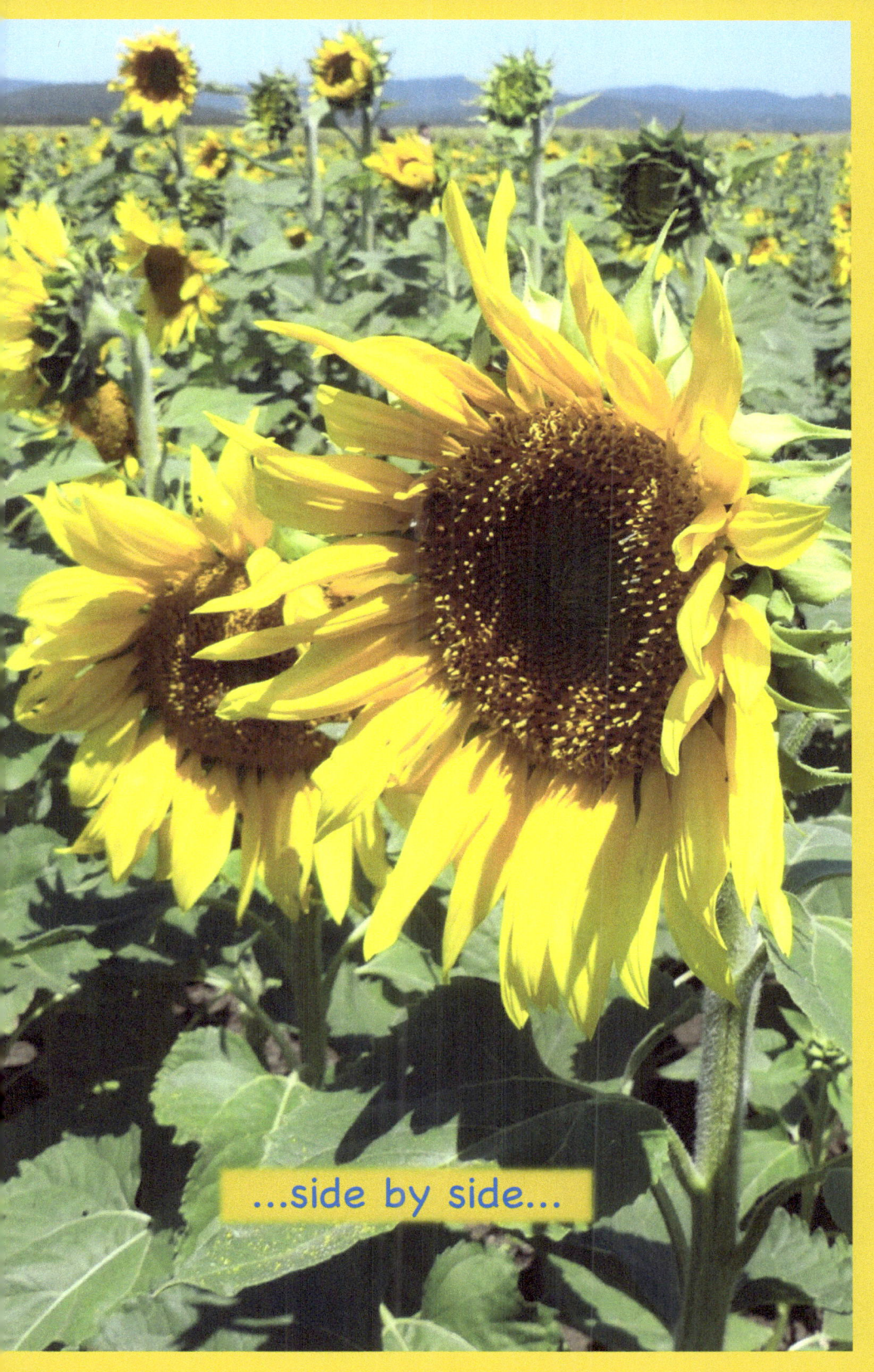

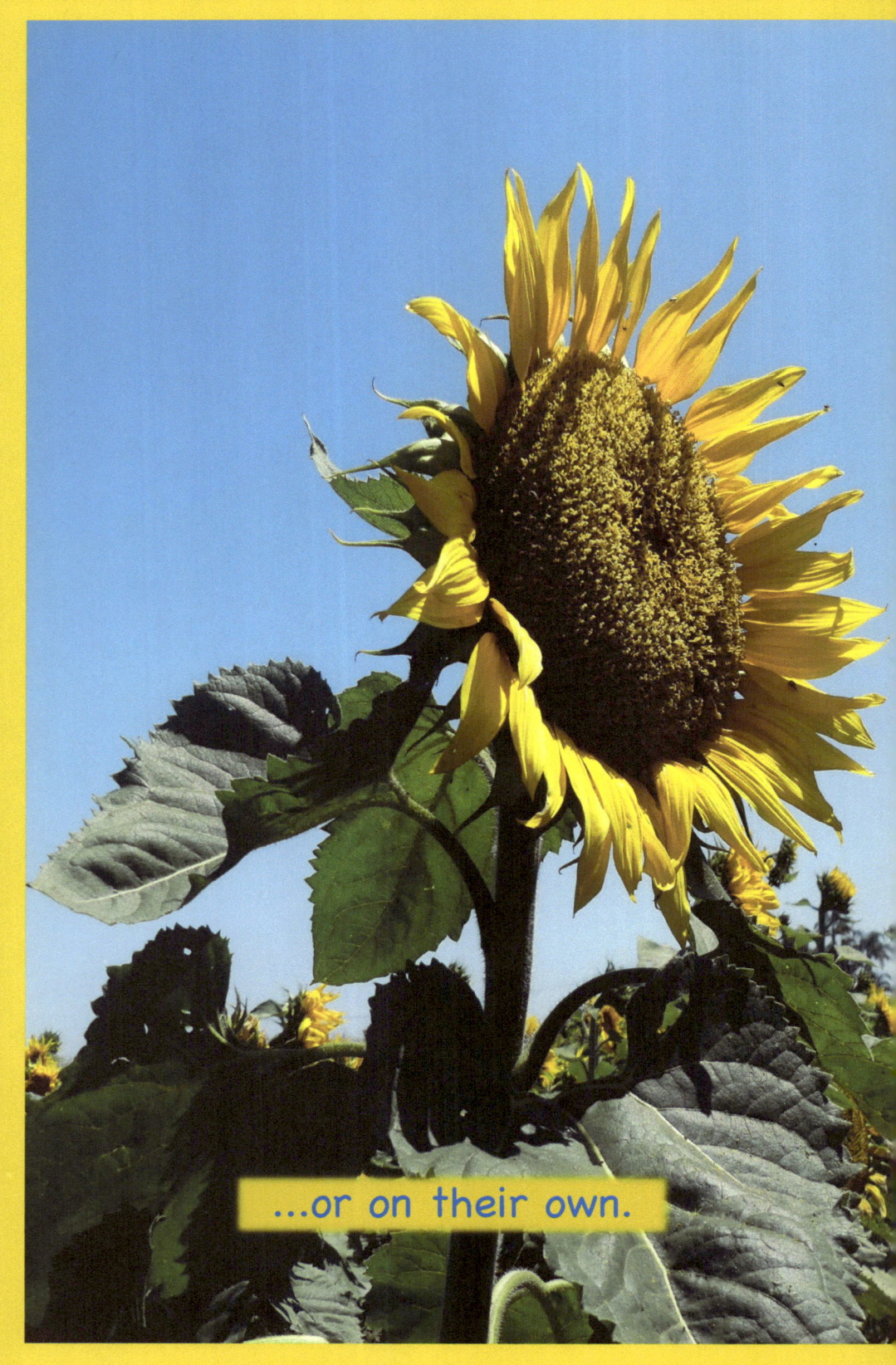

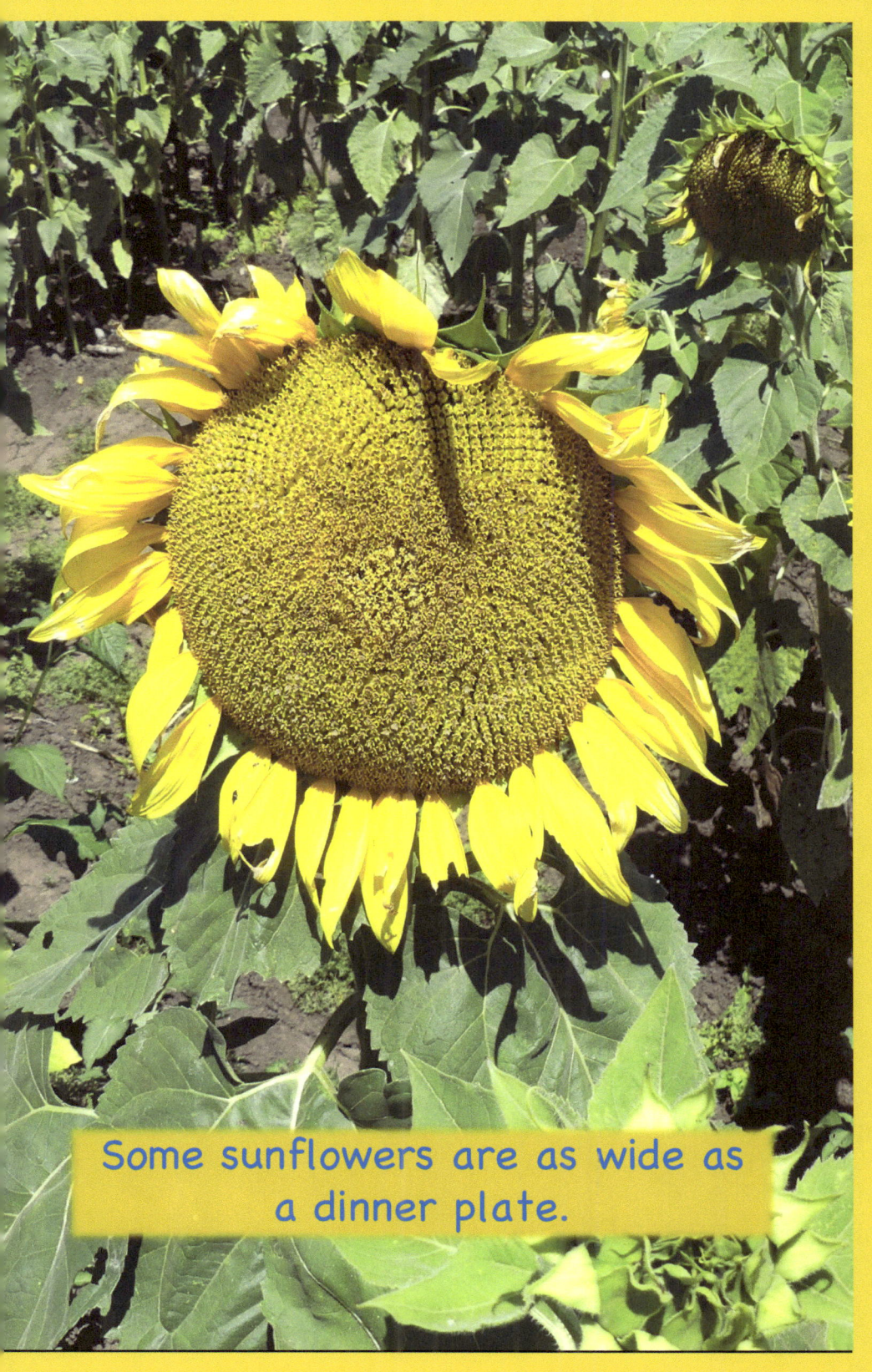
Some sunflowers are as wide as a dinner plate.

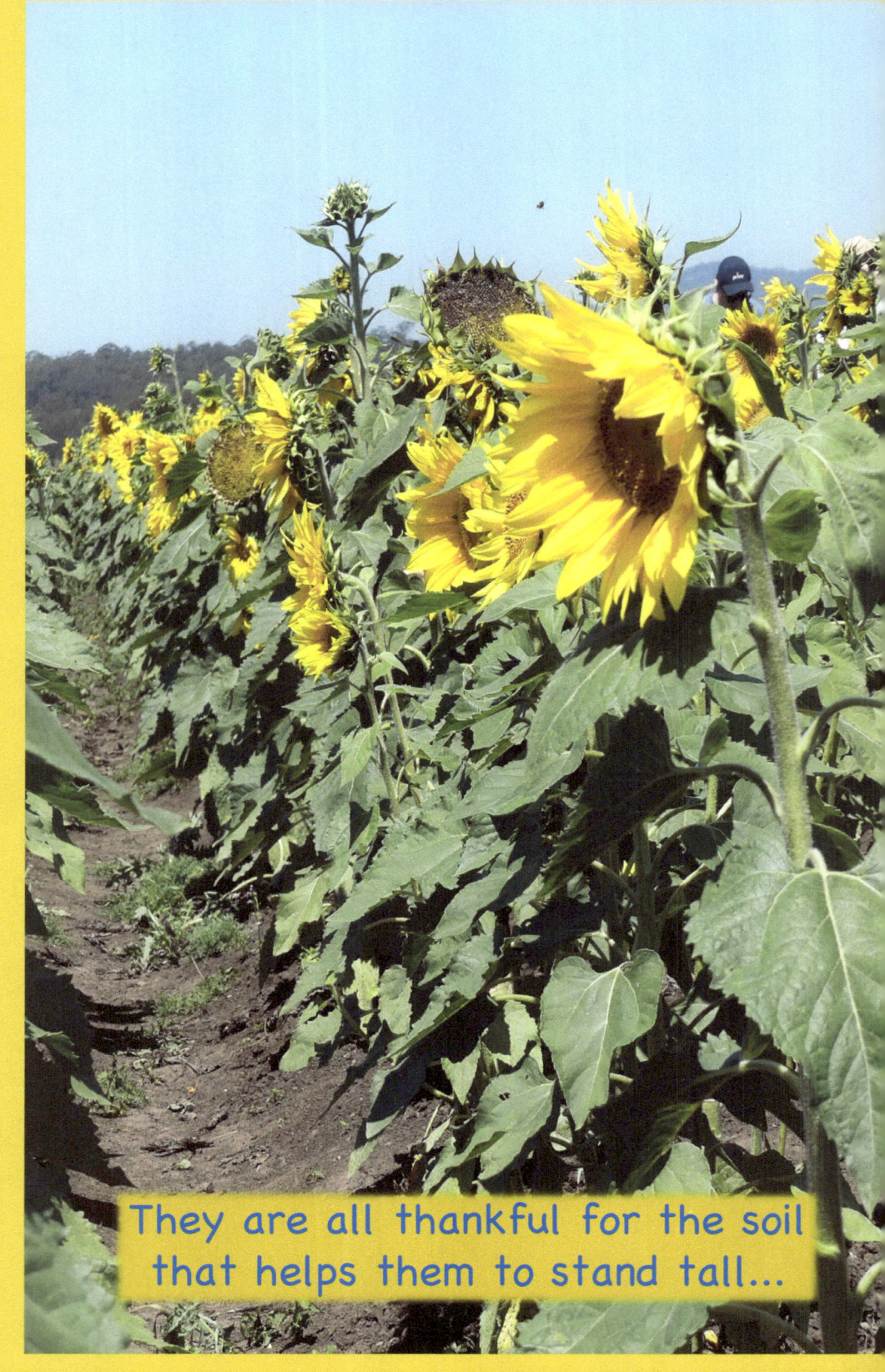
They are all thankful for the soil that helps them to stand tall...

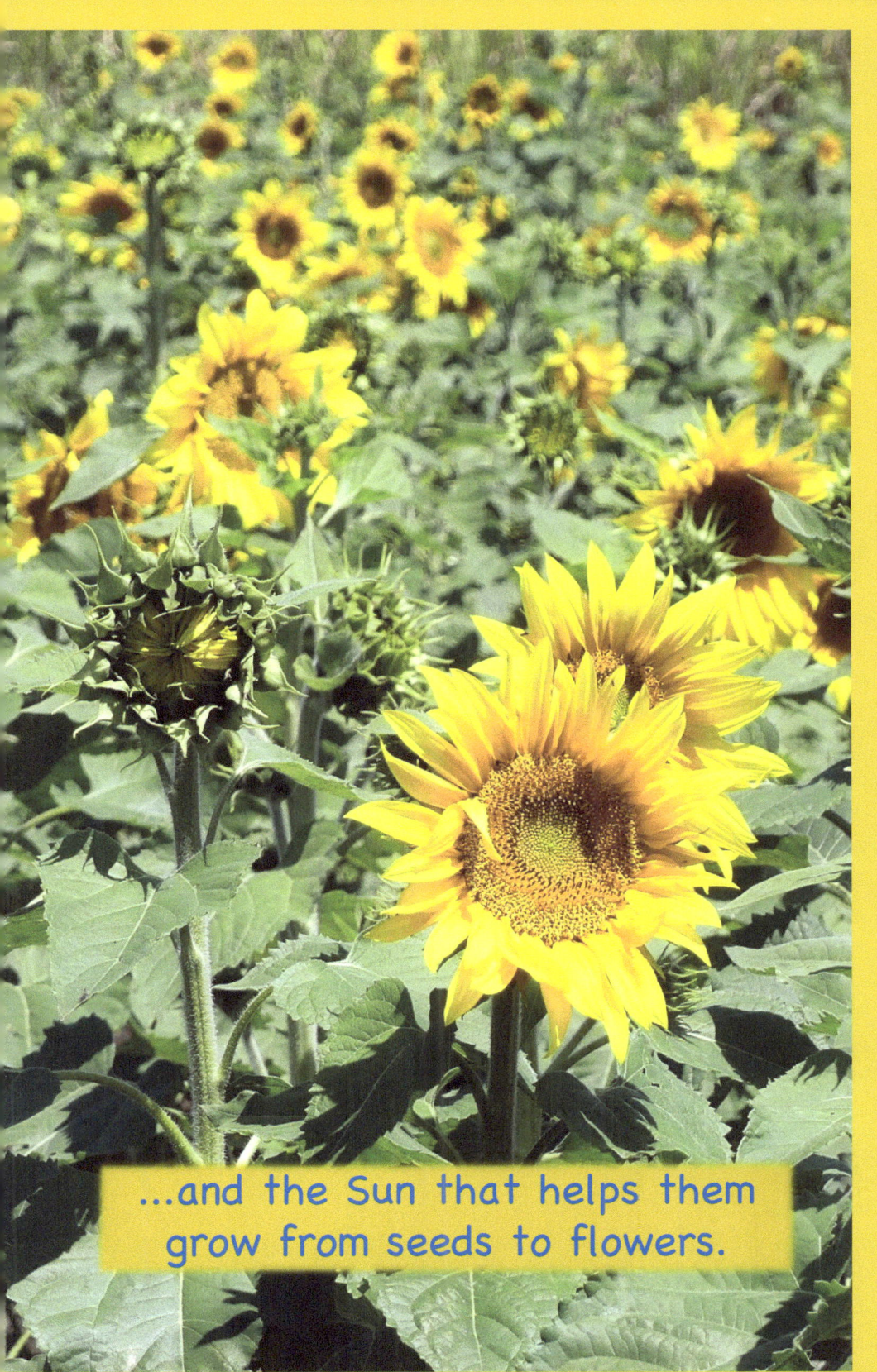

...and the Sun that helps them grow from seeds to flowers.

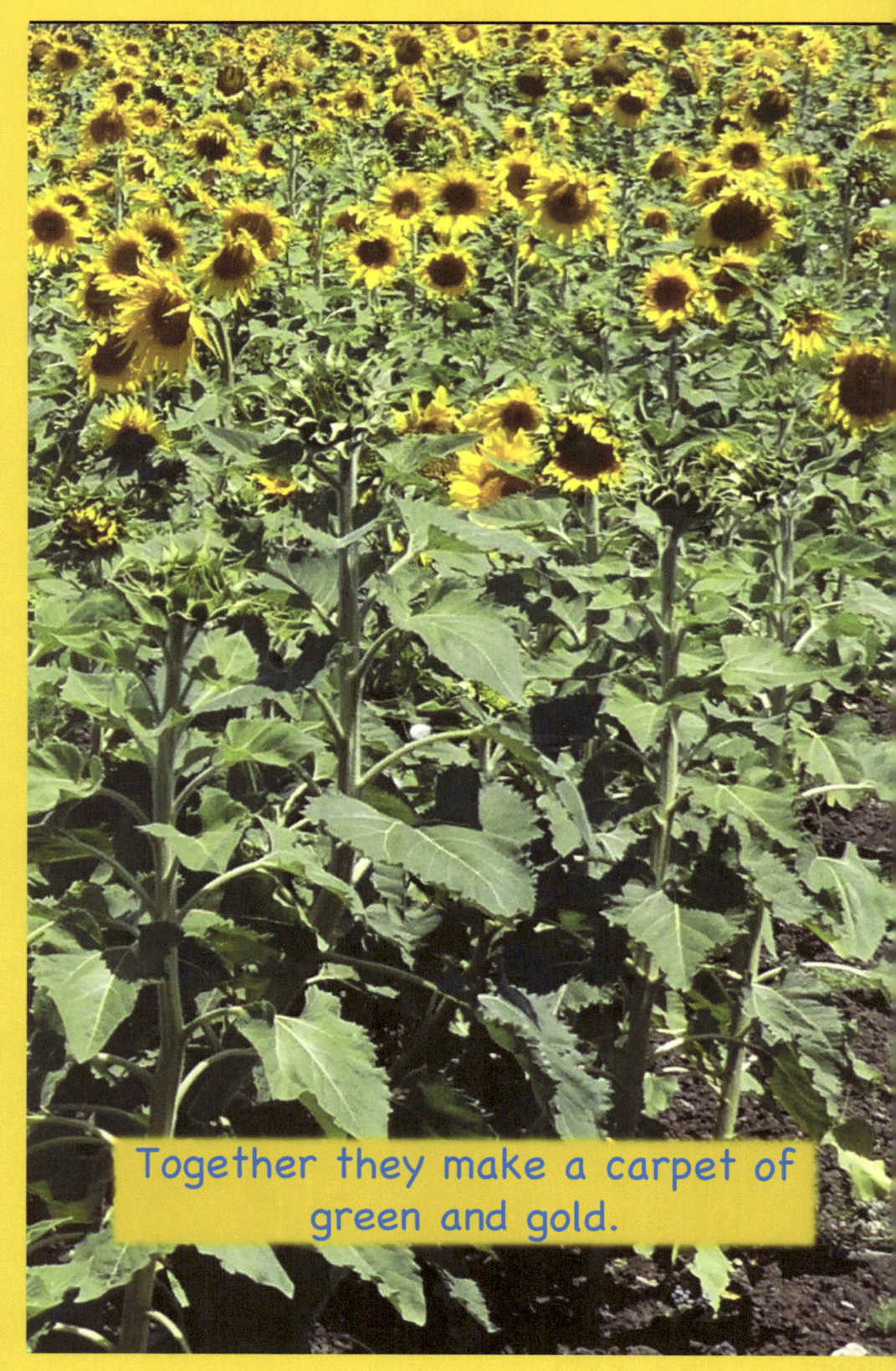

Together they make a carpet of green and gold.

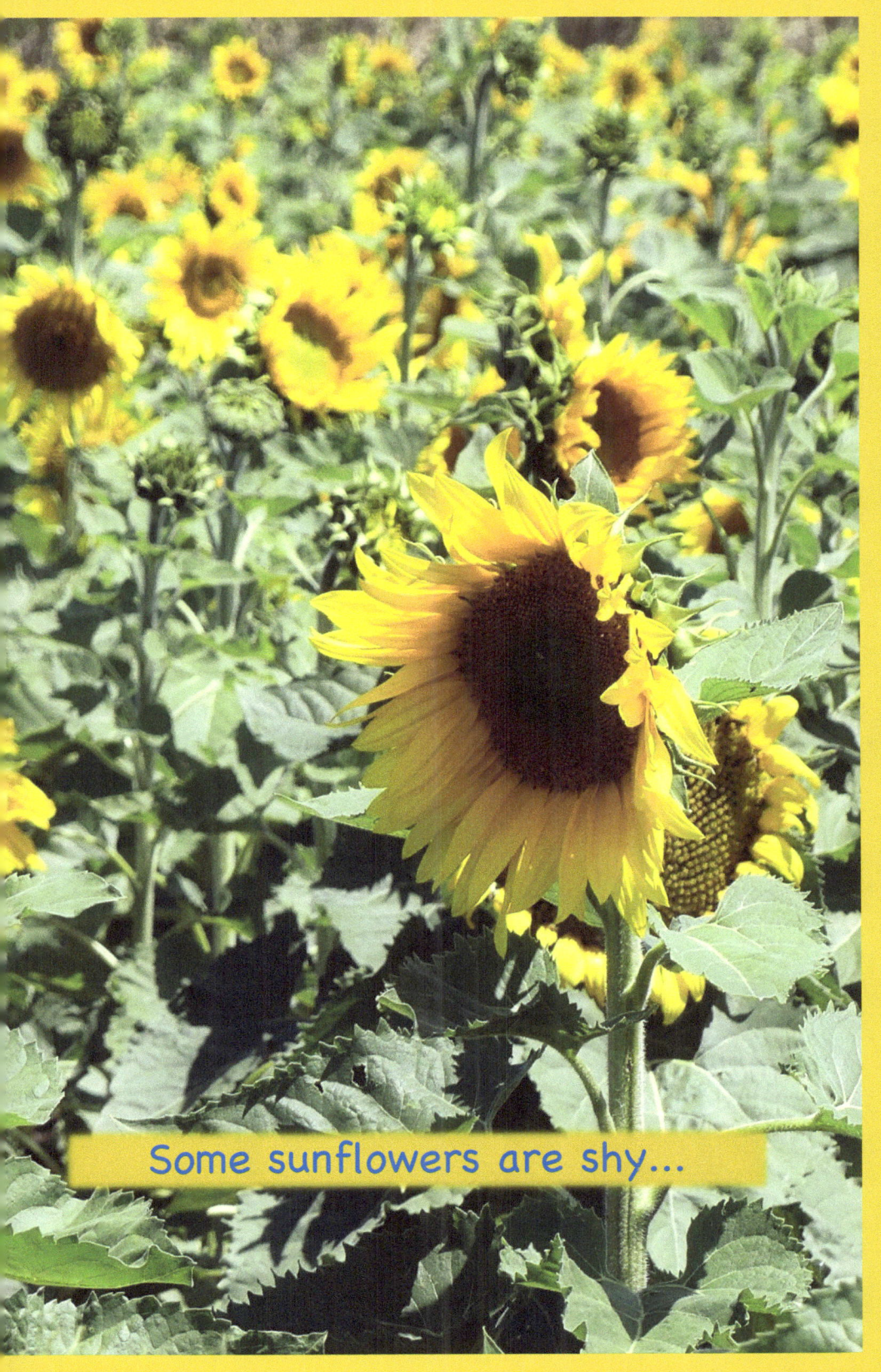
Some sunflowers are shy...

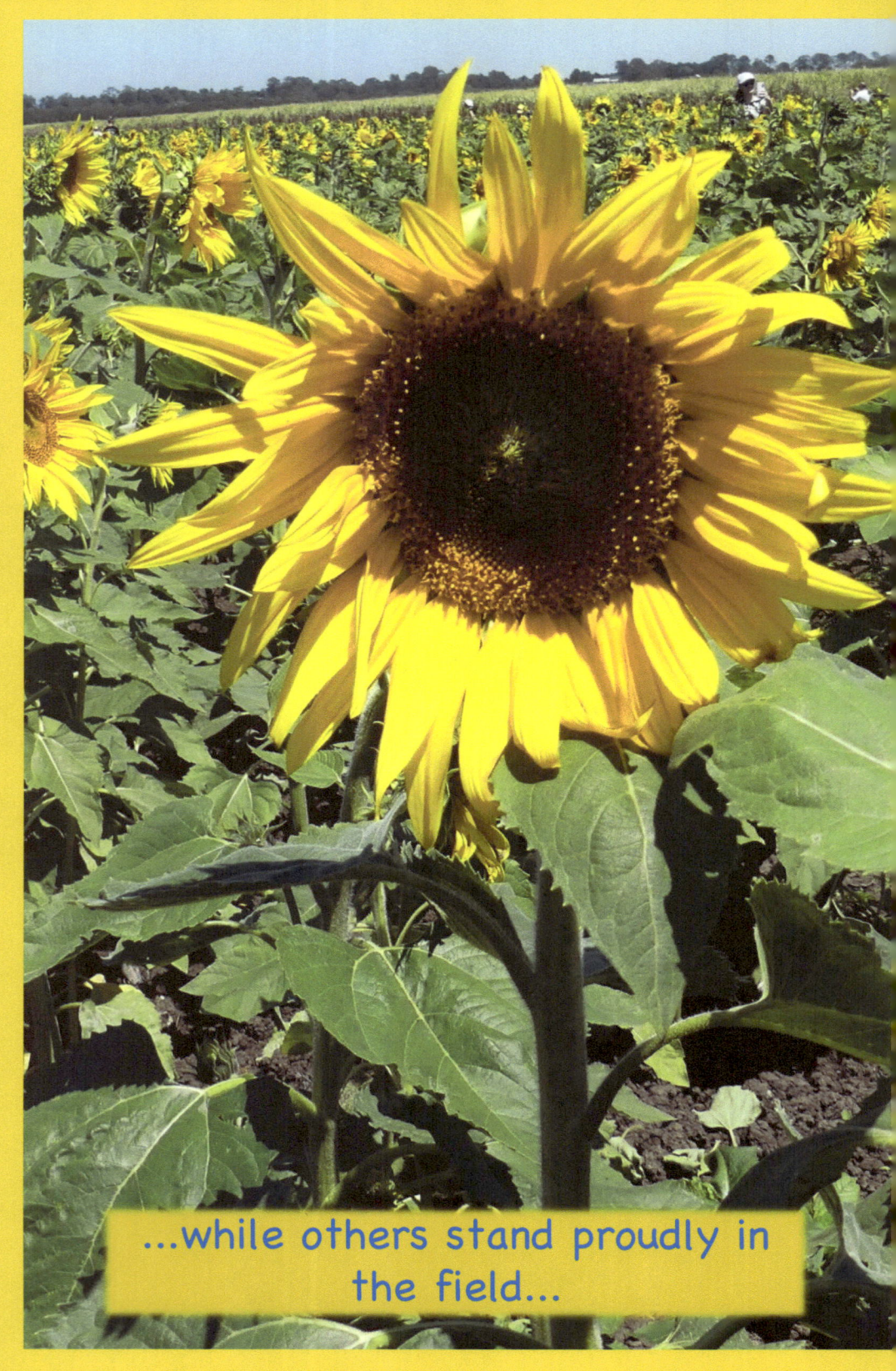
...while others stand proudly in the field...

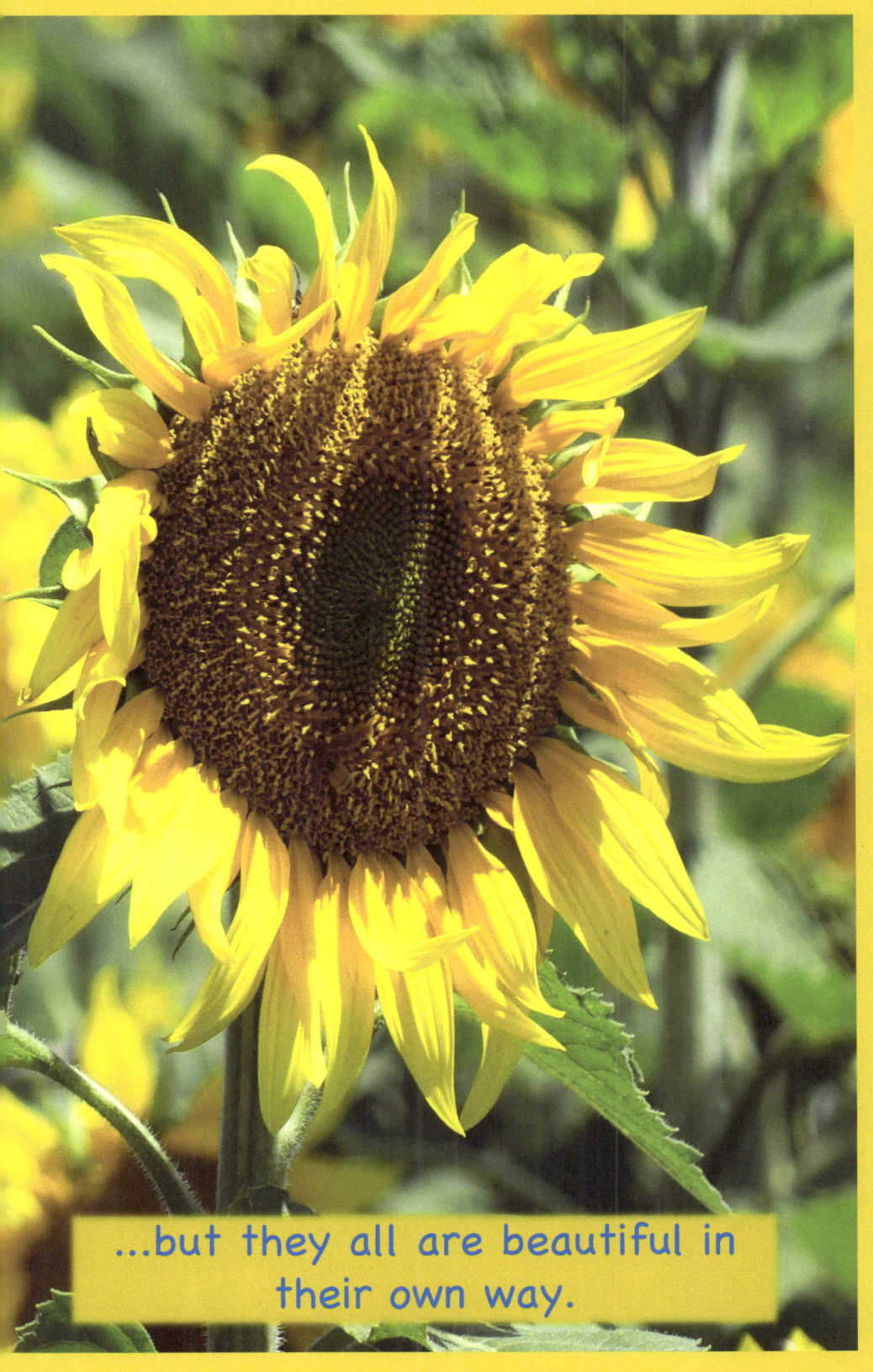

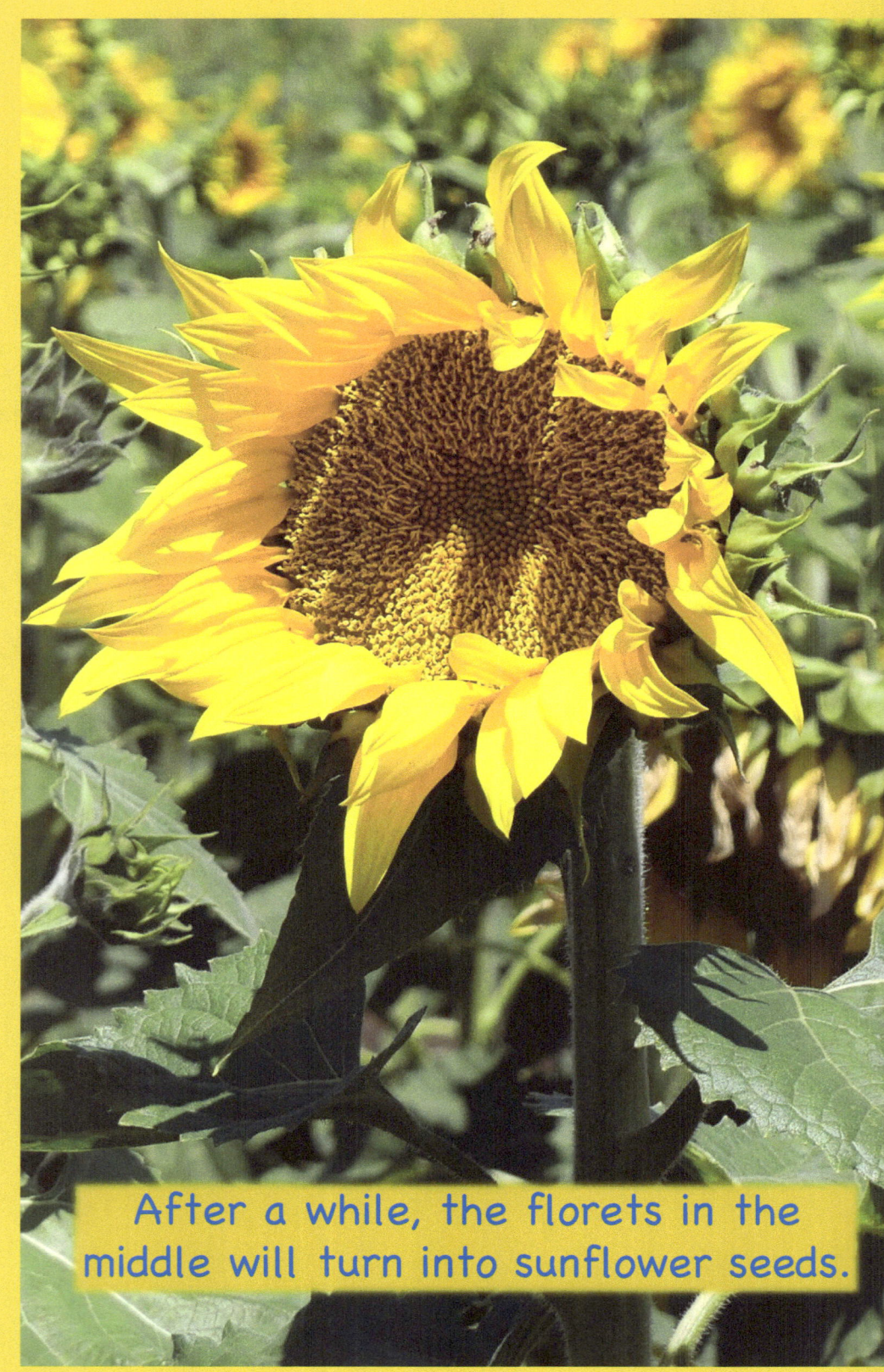

After a while, the florets in the middle will turn into sunflower seeds.

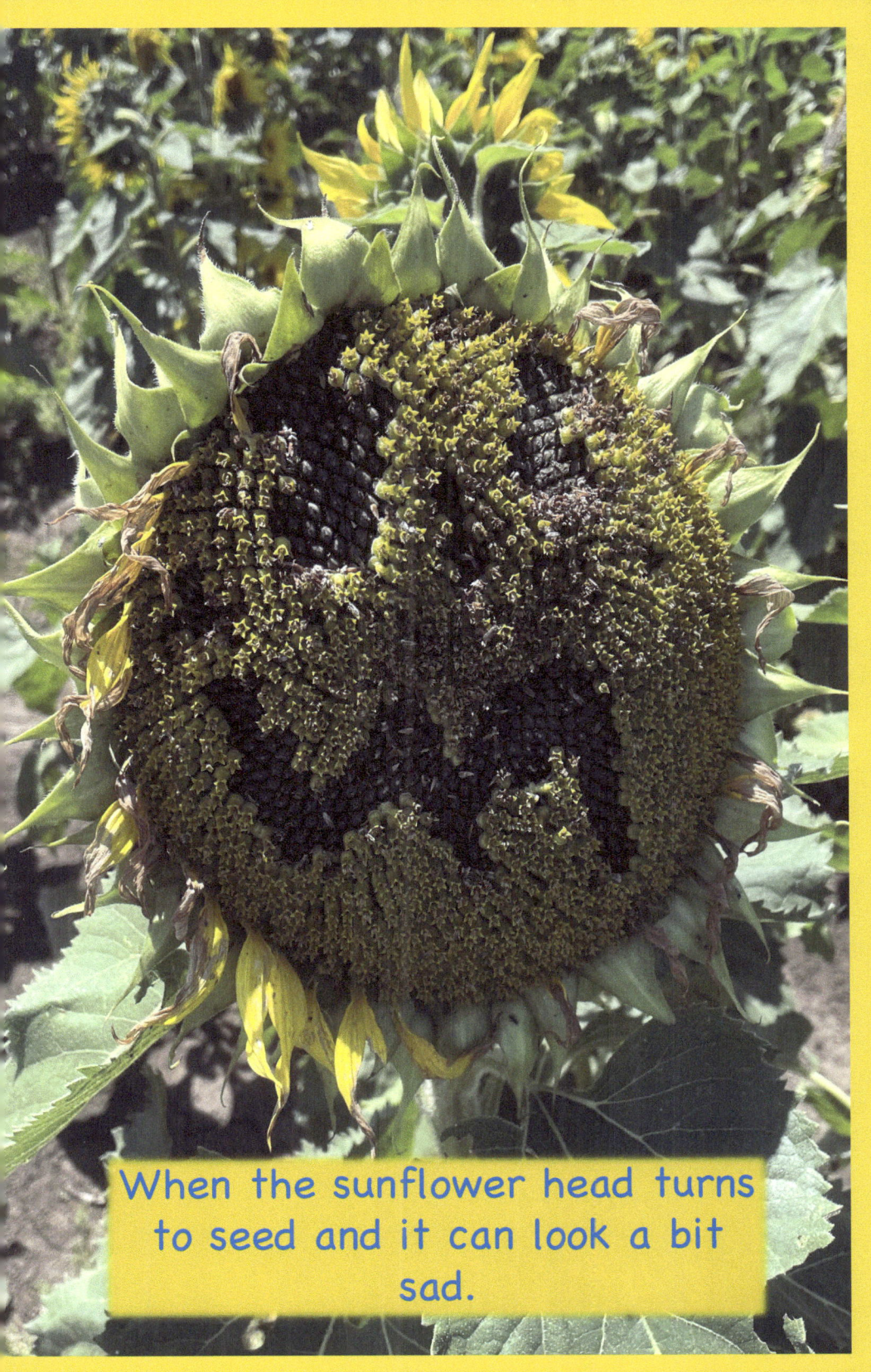

When the sunflower head turns to seed and it can look a bit sad.

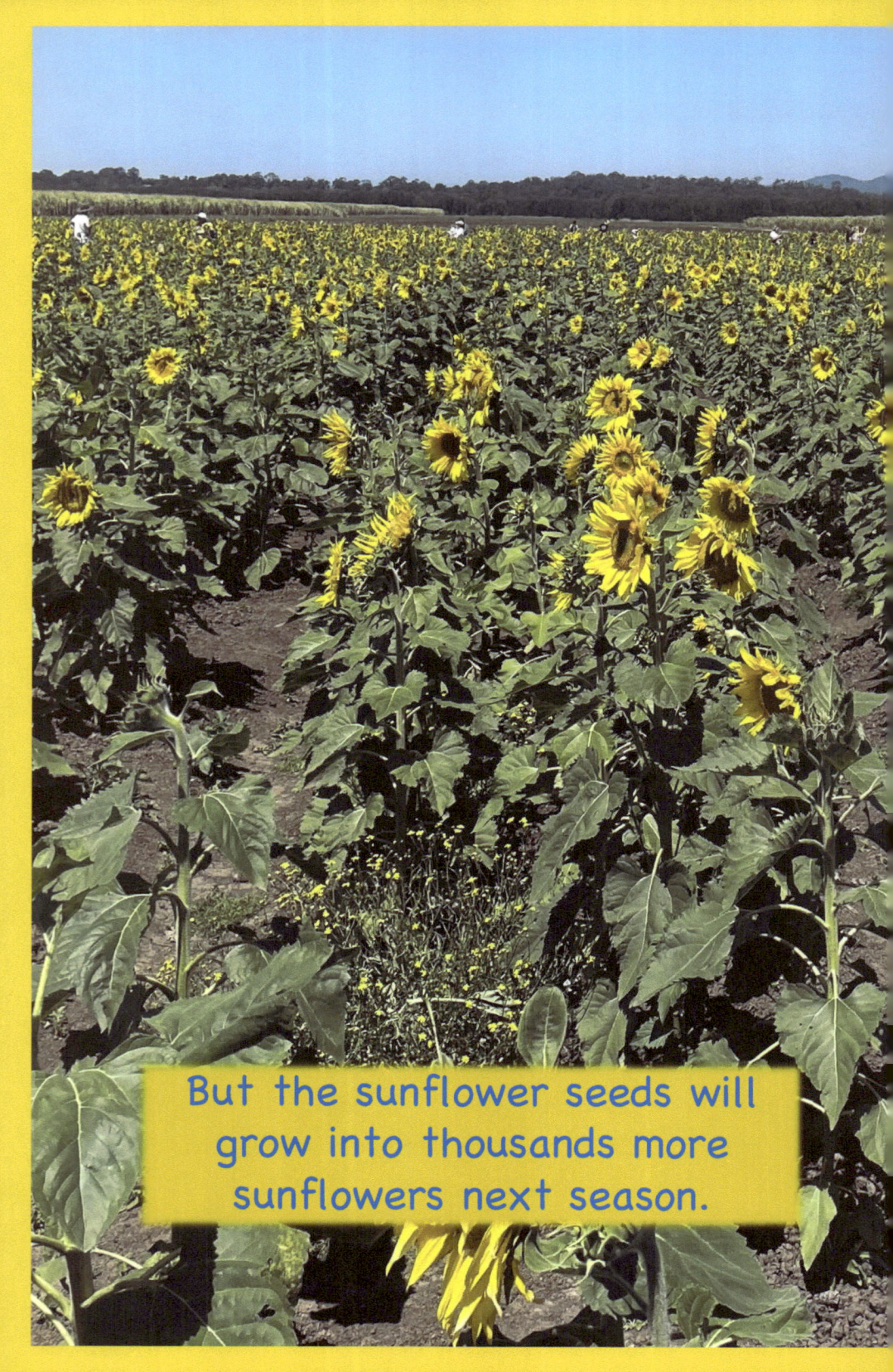

But the sunflower seeds will grow into thousands more sunflowers next season.

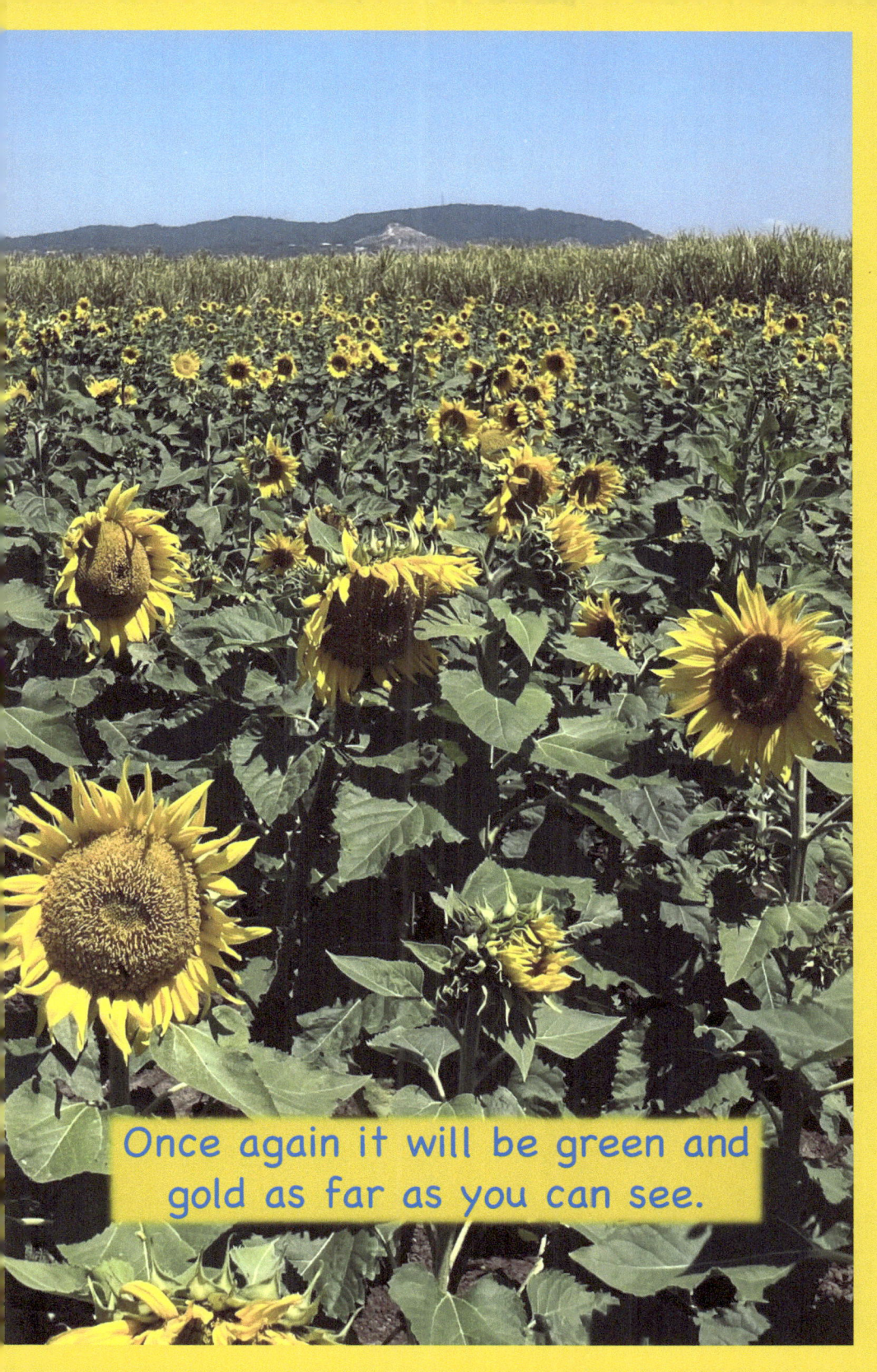
Once again it will be green and gold as far as you can see.

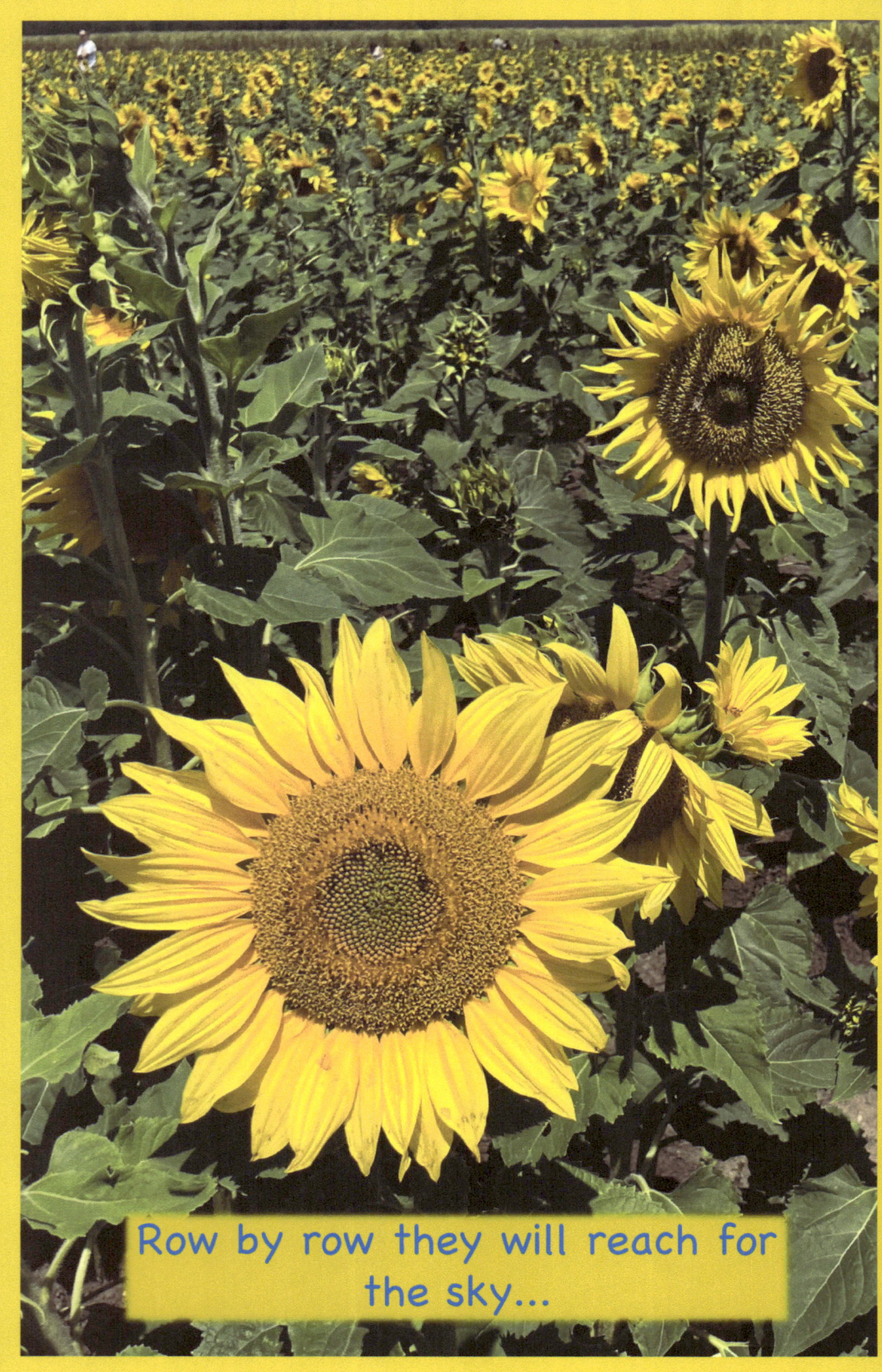

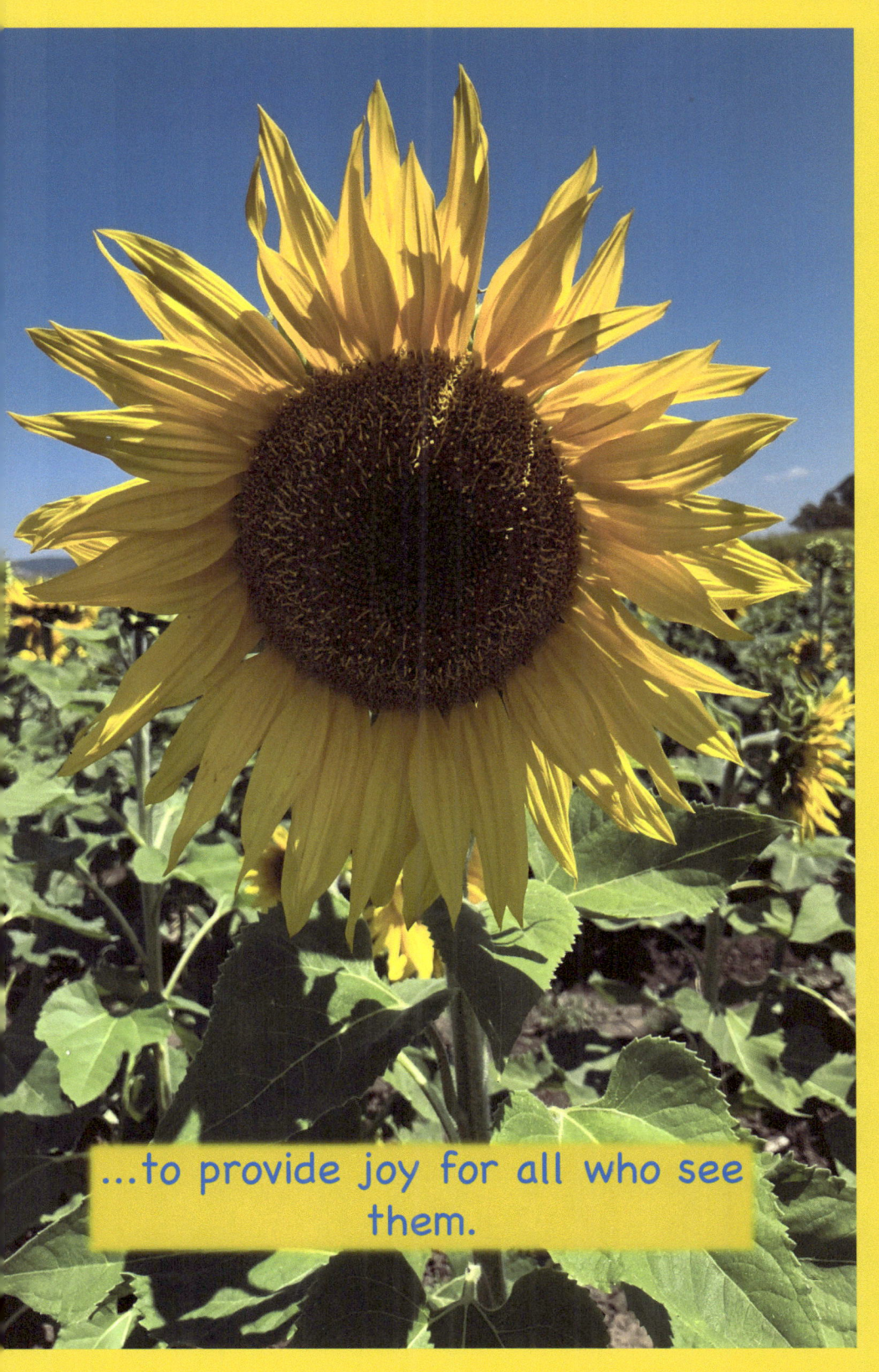
...to provide joy for all who see them.

Other titles in this series are also available at Amazon in Kindle or paperback format.

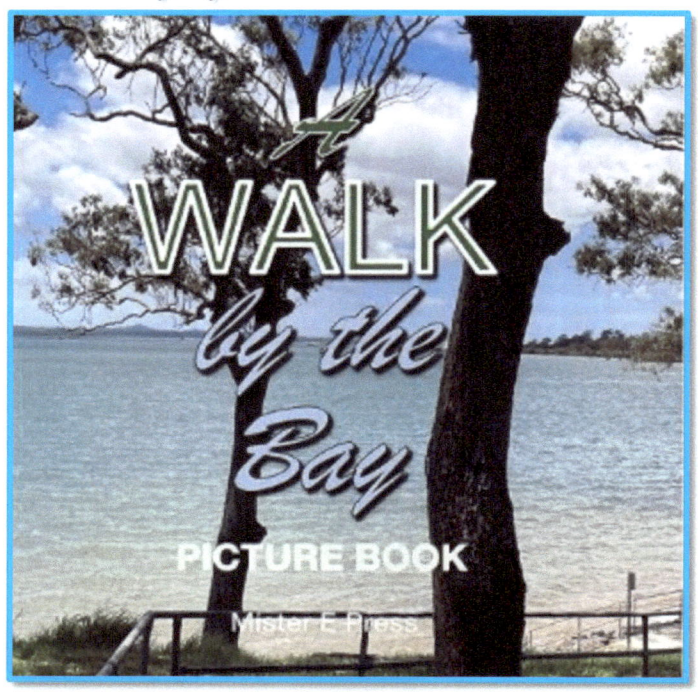

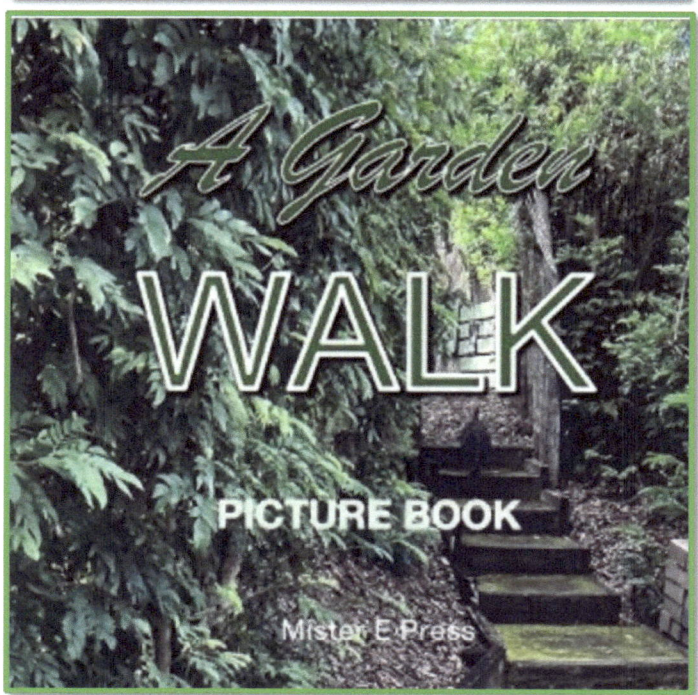

www.ingramcontent.com/pod-product-compliance
Lightning Source LLC
Chambersburg PA
CBHW040253220526
45473CB00001B/470